Math in F☉CUS®

Singapore Math®
by Marshall Cavendish

Extra Practice and Homework

Program Consultant
Dr. Fong Ho Kheong

Authors
Chelvi Ramakrishnan
Michelle Choo

Marshall Cavendish Education

U.S. Distributor

Houghton Mifflin Harcourt.
The Learning Company™

Grade **3B**

© 2020 Marshall Cavendish Education Pte Ltd

Published by Marshall Cavendish Education
Times Centre, 1 New Industrial Road, Singapore 536196
Customer Service Hotline: (65) 6213 9688
US Office Tel: (1-914) 332 8888 | Fax: (1-914) 332 8882
E-mail: cs@mceducation.com
Website: www.mceducation.com

Distributed by
Houghton Mifflin Harcourt
125 High Street
Boston, MA 02110
Tel: 617-351-5000
Website: www.hmhco.com/programs/math-in-focus

First published 2020

Marshall Cavendish® and *Math in Focus*® are registered trademarks of Times Publishing Limited.

Singapore Math® is a trademark of Singapore Math Inc.® and Marshall Cavendish Education Pte Ltd.

ISBN 978-0-358-10303-5

Printed in Singapore

4 5 6 7 8 9 10   1401   26 25 24 23 22
4500840209   B C D E F

The cover image shows a llama.
Llamas live in herds on the mountains of South America.
A baby llama is called a cria.
Like horses and donkeys, llamas are often used to transport goods.
Llamas are intelligent animals and they can learn simple tasks or instructions quickly.
Their soft wool can be used to make warm clothes like scarves and sweaters.

Contents

© 2020 Marshall Cavendish Education Pte Ltd

Preface

Welcome!

Math in **Focus**®: Singapore Math® *Extra Practice and Homework* is written to be used with the **Math** in **Focus**®: Singapore Math® *Student Edition*, to support your learning.

This book provides activities and problems that closely follow what you have learned in the Student Edition.

- In **Activities**, you practice the concepts and skills you learned in the Student Edition, so that you can master the concepts and build your confidence.

- In **MATH JOURNAL**, you reflect on your thinking when you write down your thoughts about the math concepts you learned.

- In **PUT ON YOUR THINKING CAP!**, you develop your problem-solving and critical thinking skills, and challenge yourself to apply concepts in different ways.

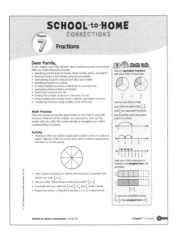

This book also includes **SCHOOL**-to-**HOME CONNECTIONS**. Each family letter summarizes the learning objectives and the key mathematical vocabulary you are using. The letter also includes one or more activities that your family can do with you to support your learning further.

BLANK

SCHOOL-to-HOME
CONNECTIONS

Chapter 7

Fractions

Dear Family,

In this chapter, your child will learn about fractions as parts of one whole. Skills your child will practice include:

- identifying unit fractions for halves, thirds, fourths, sixths, and eighths
- showing fractions and wholes using fraction models
- representing fractions using fraction discs and models
- identifying fractions of a whole
- showing fractions as points or distances on a number line
- expressing whole numbers as fractions
- identifying fractions of a set
- finding the number of items in a fraction of a set
- using models and number lines to identify equivalent fractions
- comparing fractions using models of the same size

Math Practice

There are numerous real-life opportunities for your child to work with fractions. At the end of this chapter, you may want to carry out this activity with your child. This activity will help to strengthen your child's understanding of fractions.

Activity

- Have your child use a plate or pizza pan to draw a circle on a piece of paper. Help your child cut out the circle; fold it to make 8 equal pieces; and then cut out the pieces.

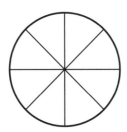

- Take 2 pieces and ask your child to write a fraction to represent the portion you took. ($\frac{2}{8}$ or $\frac{1}{4}$)
- Ask your child: "What fraction of the pizza is left?" ($\frac{6}{8}$ or $\frac{3}{4}$)
- Conclude with your child that $\frac{2}{8}$ and $\frac{6}{8}$, or $\frac{1}{4}$ and $\frac{3}{4}$, make 1 whole.
- Repeat the activity, cutting the circle into 2, 3, 4, or 6 equal pieces.

Math Talk

Discuss **equivalent fractions** with your child. For example,

$$\frac{1}{3} = \frac{2}{6}$$

Use number lines to help your child recognize that $\frac{1}{2}$, $\frac{2}{4}$, and $\frac{4}{8}$ are equivalent fractions because they name the same parts of a whole.

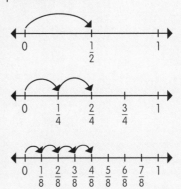

BLANK

Fill in each missing fraction.

5

$\frac{1}{3}$ and $\frac{2}{3}$ make 1 whole.

6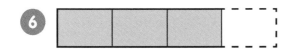

$\frac{3}{4}$ and $\frac{1}{4}$ make 1 whole.

Fill in each blank on the number line.

7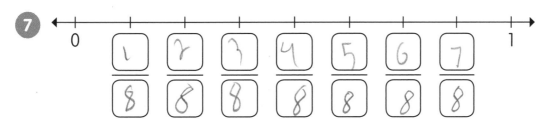

$\frac{1}{8}$ $\frac{2}{8}$ $\frac{3}{8}$ $\frac{4}{8}$ $\frac{5}{8}$ $\frac{6}{8}$ $\frac{7}{8}$

8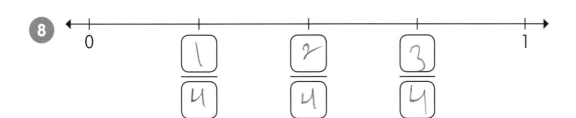

$\frac{1}{4}$ $\frac{2}{4}$ $\frac{3}{4}$

Mark an X and label each fraction on the number line.

9 a $\dfrac{1}{2}$

b $\dfrac{5}{2}$

10 a $\dfrac{4}{6}$

b $\dfrac{7}{6}$

c $\dfrac{11}{6}$

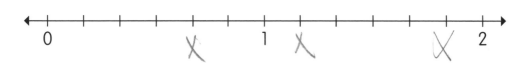

Express each of the following as a fraction.

11

3 wholes = $\dfrac{3}{1}$

12

4 wholes = $\dfrac{4}{1}$

Extra Practice and Homework Grade 3B

Chapter 7

Extra Practice and Homework
Fractions

Activity 3 Fractions as Part of a Set

Fill in each blank.

1 What fraction of the cupcakes have a ribbon on them?

$\dfrac{6}{8}$ of the cupcakes have a ribbon on them.

2 What fraction of the balls are rugby balls?

$\dfrac{4}{6}$ of the balls are rugby balls.

3 What fraction of the dragonflies are small?

$\dfrac{3}{4}$ of the dragonflies are small.

4 What fraction of the ants are big?

$\dfrac{3}{6}$ of the ants are big.

5 What fraction of the eggs have been hatched into chicks?

$\dfrac{2}{3}$ of the eggs have been hatched into chicks.

6 What fraction of the ducklings are in the pond?

$\dfrac{3}{4}$ of the ducklings are in the pond.

7 What fraction of the people are adults?

$\dfrac{5}{8}$ of the people are adults.

8 What fraction of the birds are in the nest?

$\dfrac{4}{8}$ of the birds are in the nest.

Use the pictures to help you answer each question.

9

$\frac{1}{2}$ of 6 = _____

$\frac{1}{3}$ of 6 = _____

$\frac{1}{6}$ of 6 = _____

10

$\frac{1}{2}$ of 8 = _____

$\frac{1}{4}$ of 8 = _____

$\frac{1}{8}$ of 8 = _____

11

$\dfrac{1}{2}$ of 12 = _____

$\dfrac{1}{3}$ of 12 = _____

$\dfrac{1}{4}$ of 12 = _____

$\dfrac{1}{6}$ of 12 = _____

Find the value of each of the following.
Draw a bar model to help you.

12 $\dfrac{1}{3}$ of 21 = _____

13 $\dfrac{3}{4}$ of 20 = _____

14 $\frac{5}{8}$ of 16 = _____

15 $\frac{1}{6}$ of 18 = _____

16 $\frac{3}{8}$ of 24 = _____

17 $\frac{2}{3}$ of 15 = _____

Chapter 7

Extra Practice and Homework
Fractions

Activity 4   Understanding Equivalent Fractions

Shade each model to show the equivalent fraction.
Then, write each equivalent fraction.

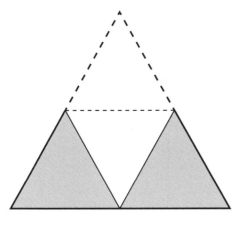 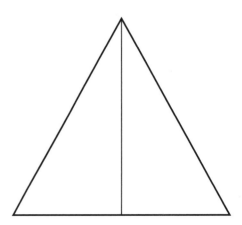

$$\frac{2}{4}$$ =   _____

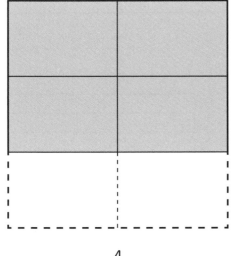 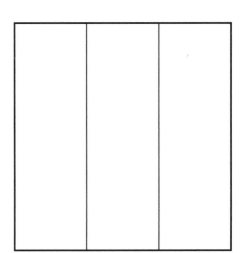

$$\frac{4}{6}$$ =   _____

3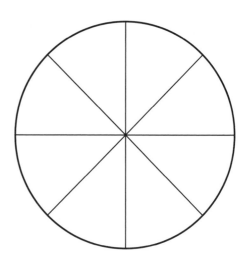

$$\frac{3}{4} \qquad = \qquad \underline{\qquad}$$

4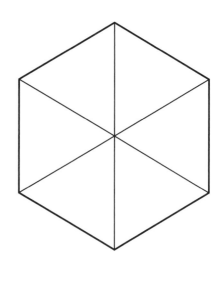

$$\frac{1}{2} \qquad = \qquad \underline{\qquad}$$

5

$$\frac{1}{4} \qquad = \qquad \underline{\qquad}$$

Cross out the fraction(s) that do not show the shaded part of each shape.

 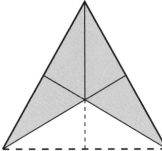

$$\frac{4}{6} \quad , \quad \frac{2}{3} \quad , \quad \frac{1}{2}$$

 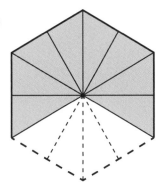

$$\frac{8}{12} \quad , \quad \frac{4}{8} \quad , \quad \frac{2}{3}$$

 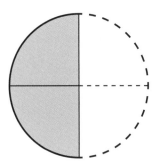

$$\frac{2}{4} \quad , \quad \frac{4}{6} \quad , \quad \frac{2}{3}$$

Fill in each missing fraction on the number lines.
Then, write the equivalent fractions.

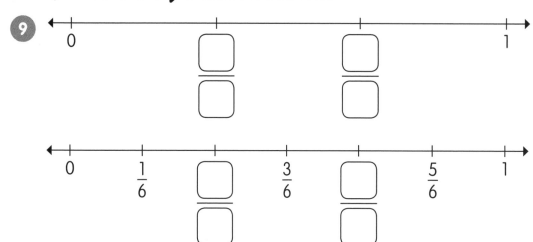

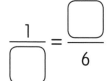

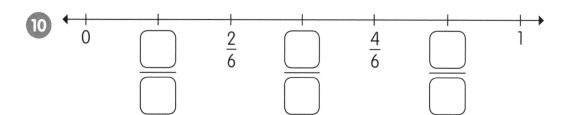

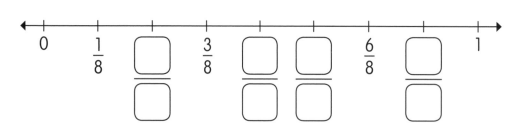

Chapter 7

Extra Practice and Homework
Fractions

Activity 5   Comparing Fractions

Shade the models to show each fraction.
Then, compare the fractions.
Write <, >, or =.

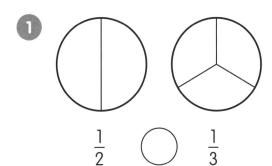

1

$\frac{1}{2}$ ◯ $\frac{1}{3}$

2

$\frac{3}{5}$ ◯ $\frac{3}{4}$

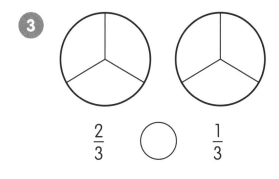

3

$\frac{2}{3}$ ◯ $\frac{1}{3}$

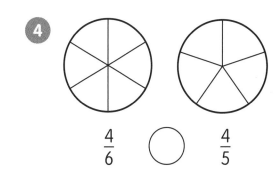

4

$\frac{4}{6}$ ◯ $\frac{4}{5}$

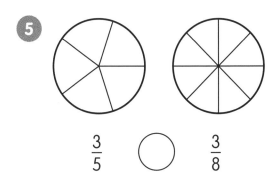

5

$\frac{3}{5}$ ◯ $\frac{3}{8}$

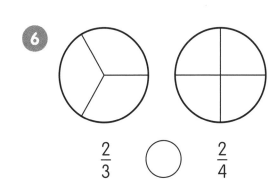

6

$\frac{2}{3}$ ◯ $\frac{2}{4}$

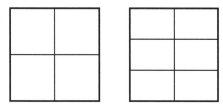

7

$$\frac{2}{4} \bigcirc \frac{2}{6}$$

8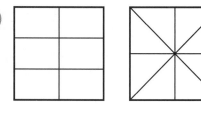

$$\frac{3}{6} \bigcirc \frac{3}{8}$$

9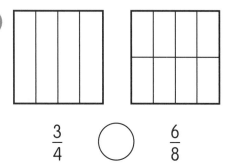

$$\frac{3}{4} \bigcirc \frac{6}{8}$$

10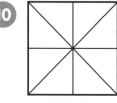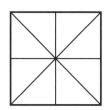

$$\frac{6}{8} \bigcirc \frac{7}{8}$$

11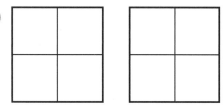

$$\frac{3}{4} \bigcirc \frac{2}{4}$$

12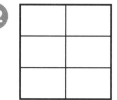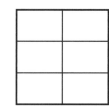

$$\frac{5}{6} \bigcirc \frac{3}{6}$$

13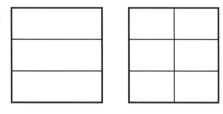

$$\frac{1}{3} \bigcirc \frac{1}{6}$$

14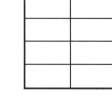

$$\frac{5}{6} \bigcirc \frac{5}{8}$$

Name: ______________________ Date: ______________

Mathematical Habit 3 Construct viable arguments

Andrea's and Ella's answers to compare $\frac{3}{4}$ and $\frac{3}{8}$ are shown below.

Andrea's answer

$\frac{3}{4} < \frac{3}{8}$

Ella's answer

$\frac{3}{4} > \frac{3}{8}$

Who is correct? Explain. Draw models to help you.

Mathematical Habit **1** Persevere in solving problems

I am a fraction.

I am greater than $\frac{1}{2}$ but less than $\frac{3}{4}$.

What fraction could I be?
Circle the fraction on the number line.

Let's find the equivalent fractions of $\frac{1}{2}$ and $\frac{3}{4}$.

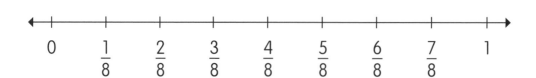

$$0 \qquad \frac{1}{8} \qquad \frac{2}{8} \qquad \frac{3}{8} \qquad \frac{4}{8} \qquad \frac{5}{8} \qquad \frac{6}{8} \qquad \frac{7}{8} \qquad 1$$

Chapter 8

Measurement

Dear Family,

In this chapter, your child will learn to measure mass and liquid volume using metric units of measurement. Skills your child will practice include:

- estimating and finding masses of objects by using different scales
- estimating and finding the volumes of liquids and capacities of containers
- converting units of measurements
- using bar models to solve 1-step real-world problems

Math Practice

There are numerous real-life opportunities for your child to measure mass, volume, and capacity. At the end of this chapter, you may want to carry out these activities with your child. These activities will help to strengthen your child's understanding of measurement.

Activity 1

- Have your child use a kitchen scale to find the mass of light objects and a bathroom scale to find the mass of heavy objects.
- Ask your child to order the masses from lightest to heaviest or heaviest to lightest.

Activity 2

- To practice working with volume, have your child record the volume of assorted beverages in your home, such as milk, juice, and bottled water.
- Have your child order the volumes from least to greatest or greatest to least.

Math Talk

Ask your child to explain metric units of mass, volume, and capacity. Help your child understand that **mass** is a measure of how heavy an object is; liquid **volume** is the amount of liquid in a container; and **capacity** is the amount of liquid a container can hold.

Mass:
kilogram (kg) and **gram (g)**
1 kg = 1,000 g

Volume and capacity:
liter (L) and **milliliter (mL)**
1 L = 1,000 mL

BLANK

22 3,400 g = _____ g + _____ g

= _____ kg _____ g

23 7,200 g = _____ g + _____ g

= _____ kg _____ g

Fill in each blank.

24 6 kg 100 g = _____ g

25 7 kg 500 g = _____ g

26 2 kg 600 g = _____ g

27 1 kg 700 g = _____ g

28 8 kg 800 g = _____ g

29 4,900 g = _____ kg _____ g

30 5,200 g = _____ kg _____ g

31 3,800 g = _____ kg _____ g

32 9,400 g = _____ kg _____ g

33 6,300 g = _____ kg _____ g

Shade the circle next to the answer.

34 What is the mass of a cellphone?

(A) 140 g

(B) 14 kg

(C) 1,400 kg

(D) 14 g

Answer each question.

35 Yong has two bags.

Which bag is heavier? Explain.

_____

_____

36

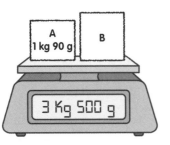

Is Box B heavier than Box A? Explain.

_____

_____

Chapter 8

Extra Practice and Homework
Measurement

Activity 2 Liquid Volume: Liters and Milliliters

Estimate the capacity of each container.
Write "more" or "less" in each blank.

1

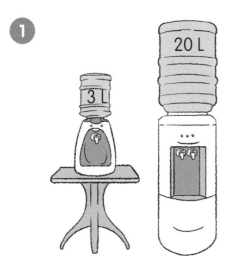

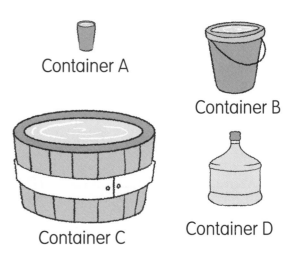

Container A

Container B

Container C

Container D

	Container	Estimated Volume
a	A	_less_ than 3 L
b	B	_less_ than 20 L
c	C	_more_ than 20 L
d	D	_more_ than 3 L

Find the volume of liquid in each container.
Then, write each volume.

2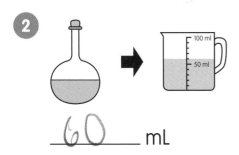

__60__ mL

3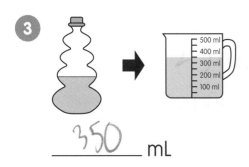

__350__ mL

4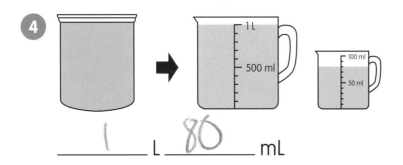

__1__ L __80__ mL

5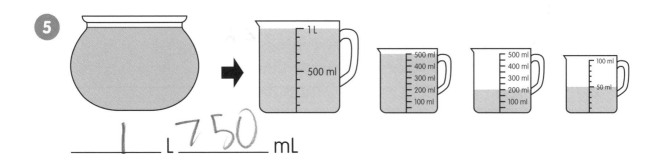

__1__ L __750__ mL

6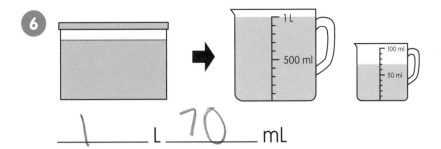

<u> 1 </u> L <u> 70 </u> mL

Draw the level of the liquid in each beaker.

7 400 mL

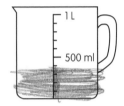

8 700 mL

9 60 mL

10 20 mL

11 350 mL

12 150 mL

Write in milliliters.

13 2 L 450 mL = __2,000__ mL + __450__ mL

   = __2,450__ mL

14 1 L 150 mL = __1,000__ mL + __150__ mL

   = __1,150__ mL

15 2 L 300 mL = __2,000__ mL + __300__ mL

   = __2,300__ mL

16 3 L 20 mL = __3,000__ mL + __20__ mL

   = __3,020__ mL

Write in liters and milliliters.

17 4,900 mL = __4,000__ mL + __900__ mL

   = __4__ L __900__ mL

18 6,550 mL = __6,000__ mL + __550__ mL

   = __6__ L __550__ mL

19 2,090 mL = __2,000__ mL + __90__ mL

   = __2__ L __90__ mL

20 7,060 mL = __7,000__ mL + __60__ mL

   = __7__ L __60__ mL

Fill in each blank.

21 **a** 1 L 400 mL = _1,400_ mL

b 5 L 60 mL = _5,060_ mL

c 4 L 20 mL = _4,020_ mL

d 6 L 300 mL = _6,300_ mL

e 8 L 240 mL = _8,240_ mL

f 7,080 mL = _7_ L _80_ mL

g 9,900 mL = _9_ L _900_ mL

h 1,050 mL = _1_ L _50_ mL

i 3,700 mL = _3_ L _700_ mL

j 8,120 mL = _8_ L _120_ mL

22 Find the capacities of Containers A, B, and C.

a

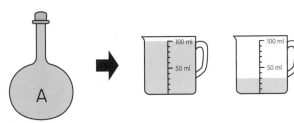

Capacity of Container A = _130_ mL

b

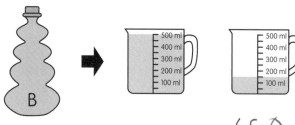

Capacity of Container B = _____650_____ mL

c

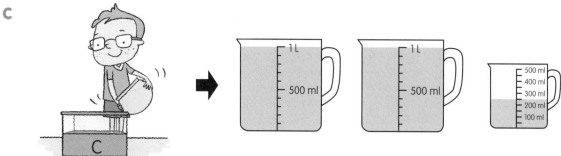

Capacity of Container C = _____2_____ L _____250_____ mL

Answer each question.

23 Which of these measurements are the same?

(a) 8 L 500 mL

b   7 L 1,500 mL

c   8,050 mL

(d) 8,500 mL

e   7,150 mL

_____

24 A tablespoon is filled with water. How much water is there?

(a) 5 mL

b   15 mL

c   50 mL

d   5 L

_____

Chapter 8

Extra Practice and Homework
Measurement

Activity 3   Real-World Problems: One-Step Problems

Solve. Show your work. Draw bar models to help you.

1   A baby elephant has a mass of 145 kilograms.
The mass of the mother elephant is 5 times heavier than the mass of the baby elephant.
What is the mass of the mother elephant?

2   A container is filled with 20 liters of syrup.
Kiri fills some bottles with syrup from the container.
Each bottle contains 2 liters of syrup.
How many bottles of syrup can he fill?

3 A watering tin contained 1 liter of water.
   Some water was used to water some plants.
   There were 350 milliliters of water left.
   How many milliliters of water were used?

4 Luis had 2 kilograms of sugar.
   He used 420 grams of it.
   What was the mass of sugar left?
   Write your answer in kilograms and grams.

5 Diego bought 800 grams of nuts on Monday.
He bought 900 grams of nuts on Tuesday.
What was the total mass of nuts that he bought?
Write your answer in kilograms and grams.

6 Ms. Smith has 8 cups of water.
Each cup contains 125 milliliters of water.
She pours all the water into a container.
How many liters of water will there be in the container?

7 The mass of a papaya was 1 kilogram.
A watermelon was 850 grams heavier than the papaya.
What was the mass of the watermelon?
Write your answer in kilograms and grams.

8 There were 1 liter 200 milliliters of water in Container A.
It had 800 milliliters more water than Container B.
How many milliliters of water were there in Container B?

Name: _____ Date: _____

Mathematical Habit 4 Use mathematical models

Write a word problem on mass and volume using the helping words and numbers given.

400	180	more	less than

Model:

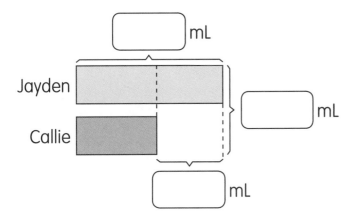

Word problem:

Mathematical Habit 4 Use mathematical models

Find the mass of each item.

lamb leg

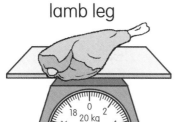

turkey   lamb leg

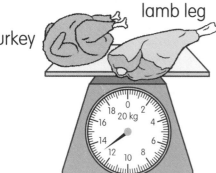

turkey   rice

a   The mass of the lamb leg is _____ kilograms.

b   The mass of the turkey is _____ kilograms.

c   The mass of the rice is _____ kilograms.

Area and Perimeter

Dear Family,

In this chapter, your child will learn about area and perimeter of plane figures. Skills your child will practice include:

• understanding the meaning of area and perimeter
• measuring areas and perimeters of plane figures
• using square units to find areas of, and using small squares to find perimeters of plane figures
• comparing areas and perimeters of two plane figures
• finding the area of rectangles using multiplication and addition
• solving real-world problems involving perimeter

Math Practice

There are numerous real-life opportunities for your child to explore the concepts of area and perimeter. At the end of this chapter, you may want to carry out this activity with your child. This activity will help to strengthen your child's understanding of area and perimeter.

Activity

• Ask your child to imagine giving a room in your home a makeover. Tell your child that you will be putting a wallpaper border around the room and putting in a carpet.
• Using a measuring tape, help your child find the length, width, and height of the room. Then, with the information, discuss how to find the floor area that is to be covered by the carpet to decide on the amount of carpeting needed, and the perimeter of the room in order to decide what length of wallpaper border to purchase.

Math Talk

Explain to your child that **perimeter** is the distance around a place figure and is measured in units such as centimeters, meters, inches, and feet. **Area** is the number of square units needed to cover the surface of a plane figure and is measured in units such as **square centimeter (cm²)**, **square meter (m²)**, **square inch (in²)**, and **square foot (ft²)**.

Help your child understand the formulas for finding area and perimeter.

Length

Width

Area of a rectangle
= **Length** × **Width**
Perimeter of a rectangle
= Length + Width + Length
  + Width

Length

Area of a square
= Length × Length
Perimeter of a square
= 4 × Length of each side

BLANK

Chapter 9

Extra Practice and Homework
Area and Perimeter

Activity 1   Area

Look at each figure and fill in each blank.

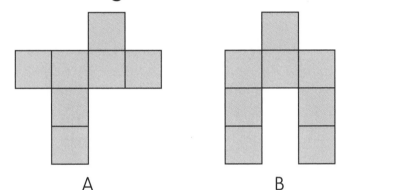

A   B   C

1 How many square tiles make each figure?

   a   The area of Figure A is made up of _____ square tiles.

   b   The area of Figure B is made up of _____ square tiles.

   c   The area of Figure C is made up of _____ square tiles.

2 Each square tile is one square unit.
What is the area of each figure?

   a   The area of Figure A is _____ square units.

   b   The area of Figure B is _____ square units.

   c   The area of Figure C is _____ square units.

3 Order the figures from the largest to the smallest area.

_____   _____   _____
   largest   smallest

Look at the figure and fill in each blank.

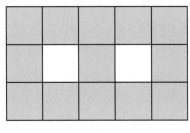

D

4 Each square tile is one square unit.
What is the area of Figure D?

The area of Figure D is _____ square units.

5 Shade squares to make a figure, E, that has an area smaller than Figure D.

The area of Figure E is _____ square units.

6 Shade squares to make a figure, F, that has an area larger than Figure D on the previous page.

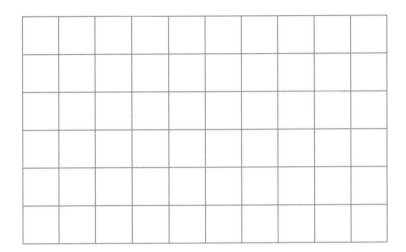

The area of Figure F is _____ square units.

Add squares to each figure to make the area of each figure 16 square units.

7

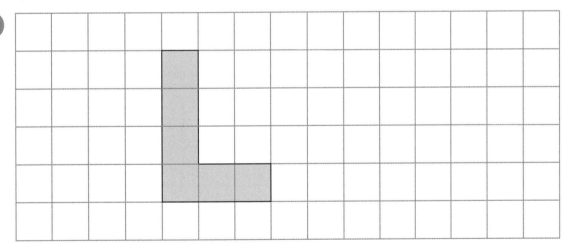

8

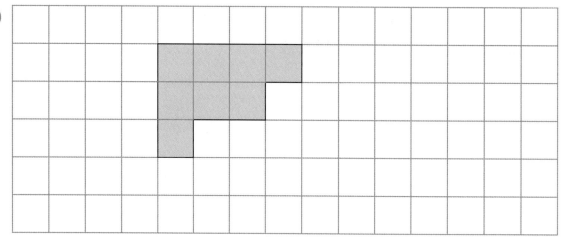

9

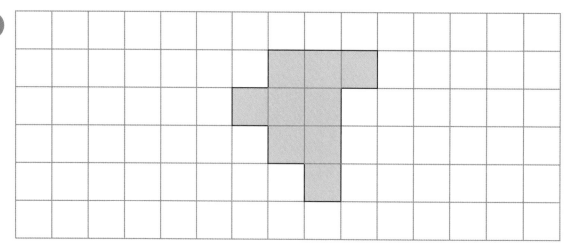

10

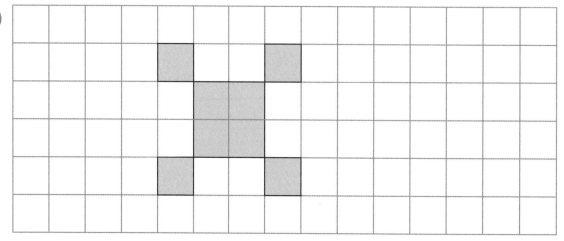

Extra Practice and Homework Grade 3B

Each figure is made up of squares and half-squares.
Look at each figure and fill in each blank.

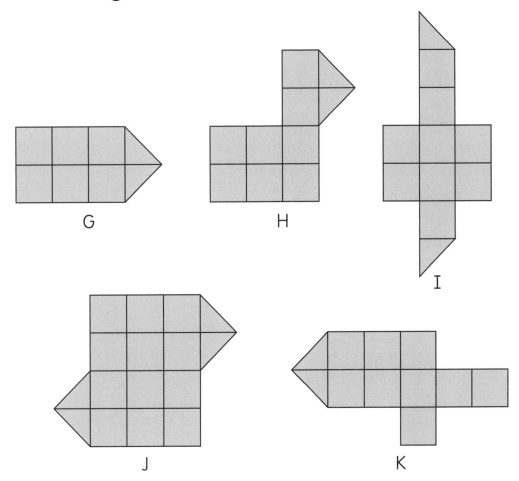

11 The area of Figure G is _____ square units.

12 The area of Figure H is _____ square units.

13 The area of Figure I is _____ square units.

14 The area of Figure J is _____ square units.

15 The area of Figure K is _____ square units.

16 Which figures have the same area?

Figures _____ and _____ have the same area.

17 Which figure has the largest area?

Figure _____ has the largest area.

18 Which figure has the smallest area?

Figure _____ has the smallest area.

Find the area of each figure.

19

The area of Figure L is _____ square units.

Then, shade squares or half-squares to form a new figure that has the same area as Figure L.

20

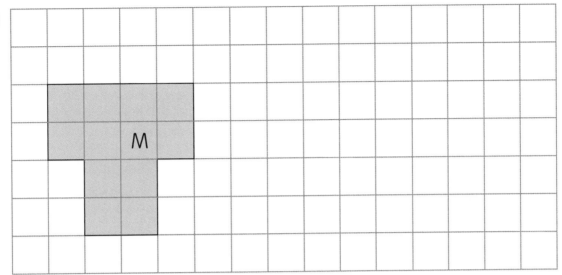

The area of Figure M is _____ square units.

Then, shade squares or half-squares to form a new figure that has an area that is larger than Figure M.

21

The area of Figure N is _____ square units.

Then, shade squares or half-squares to form a new figure that has an area that is smaller than Figure N.

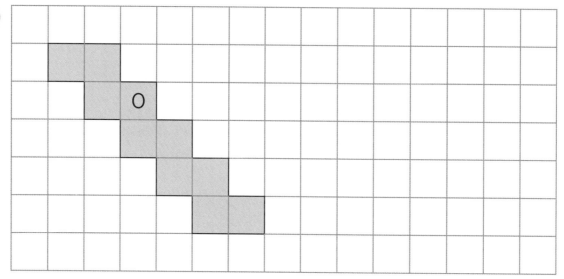

22

The area of Figure O is _____ square units.

Then, shade squares or half-squares to form a new figure that has the same area as Figure O.

Shade squares or half-squares to make figures with each given area.

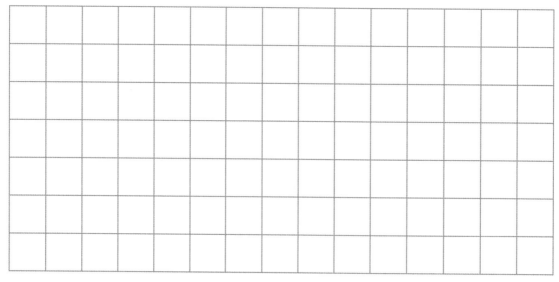

23

The area of Figure P is 8 square units.

24

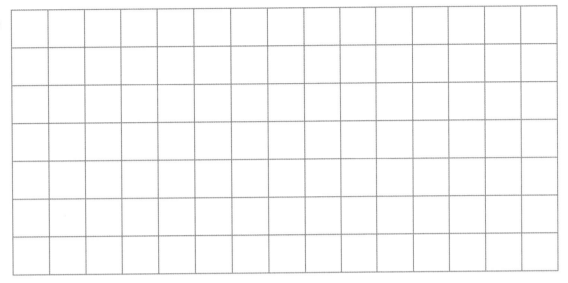

The area of Figure Q is 15 square units.

25

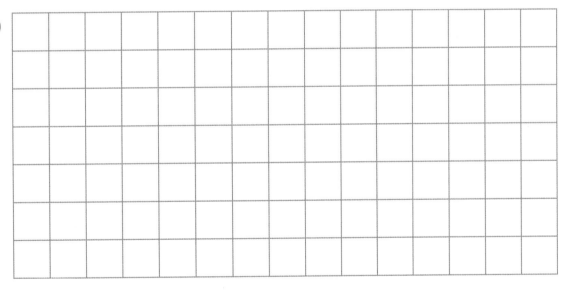

The area of Figure R is 21 square units.

26

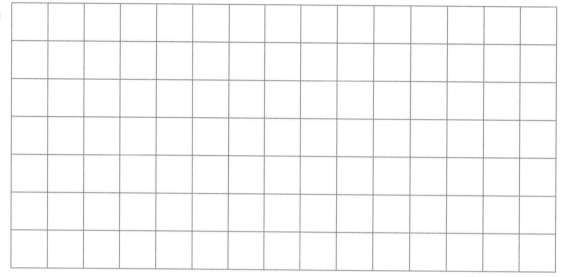

The area of Figure S is 26 square units.

27

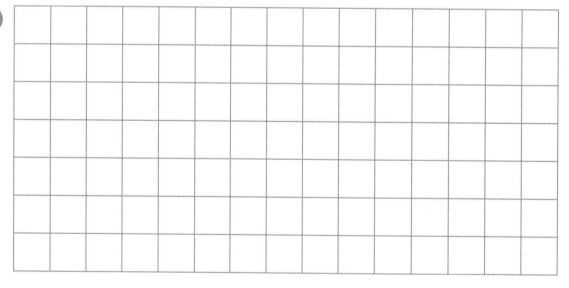

The area of Figure T is 31 square units.

Extra Practice and Homework
Area and Perimeter

Chapter 9

Activity 2   Square Units (cm² and in²)

Find the area of each figure in square centimeters (cm²).
Then, answer each question.

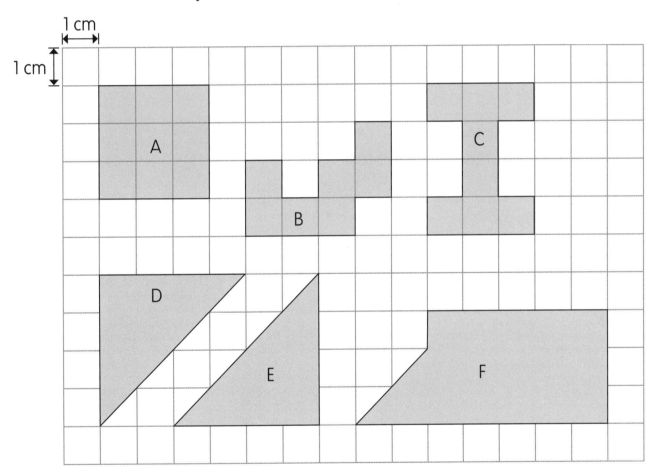

1   The area of Figure A is _____ square centimeters.

2   The area of Figure B is _____ square centimeters.

3   The area of Figure C is _____ square centimeters.

4 The area of Figure D is _____ square centimeters.

5 The area of Figure E is _____ square centimeters.

6 The area of Figure F is _____ square centimeters.

Fill in each blank.

7 Which figure has the largest area?

Figure _____ has the largest area.

8 Which figure has the smallest area?

Figure _____ has the smallest area.

9 Which figures have the same area?

Figures _____, _____, and _____ have the same area.

Add squares or half-squares to make figures with each given area.

10

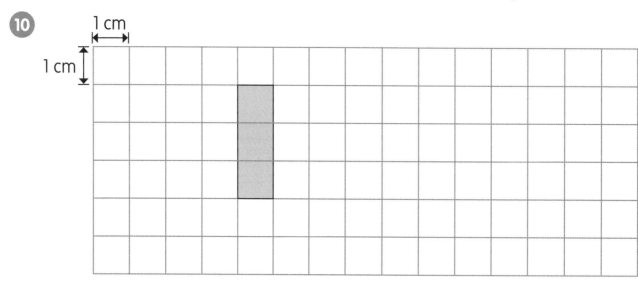

The area of the figure is 6 square centimeters.

11

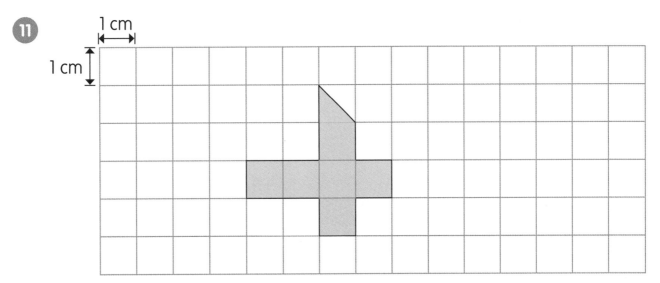

The area of the figure is 11 square centimeters.

12

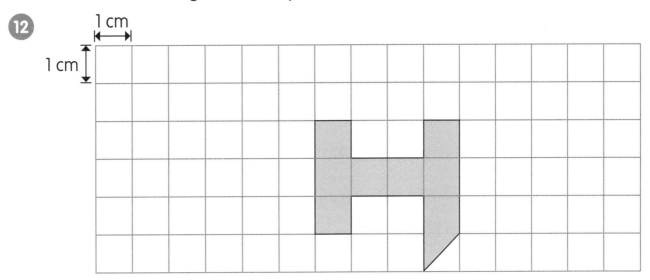

The area of the figure is 15 square centimeters.

13

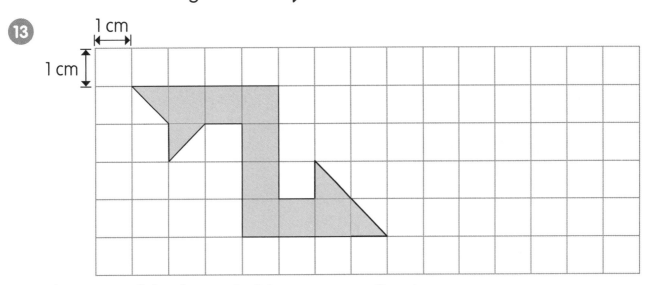

The area of the figure is 20 square centimeters.

Match each figure to its area in square inches (in²).

14 a

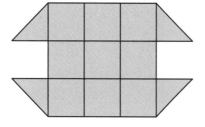

    •   • 16 in²

b

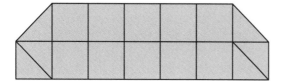

    •   • 12 in²

c

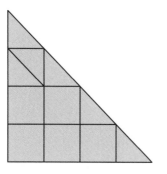

    •   • 11 in²

d

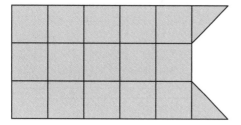

    •   • 13 in²

e

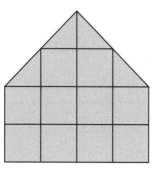

    •   • 8 in²

Find the area of each figure. Then, shade squares or half-squares to form another figure with the same area on the grid.

15

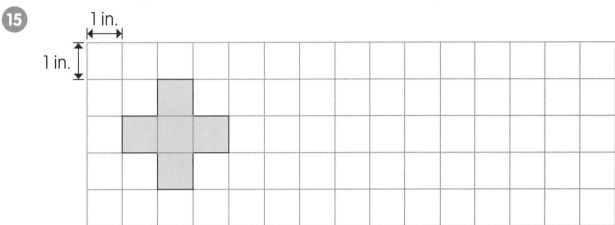

The area of the given figure is _____ square inches.

16

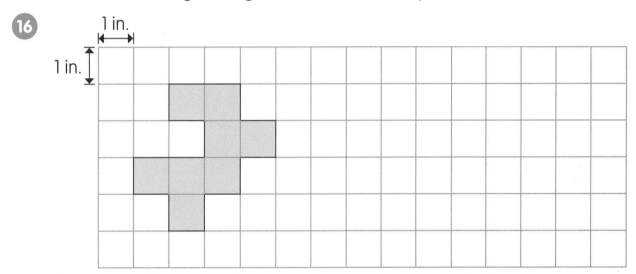

The area of the given figure is _____ square inches.

17

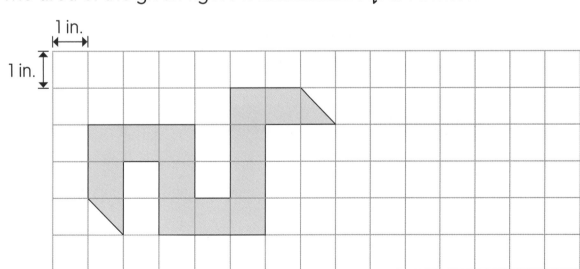

The area of the given figure is _____ square inches.

18

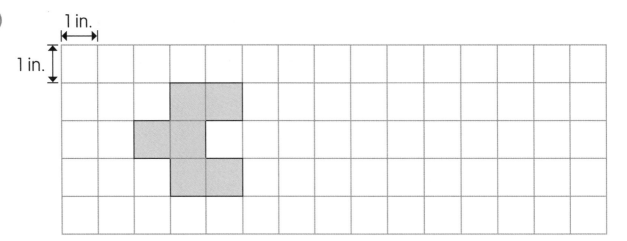

The area of the given figure is _____ square inches.

19

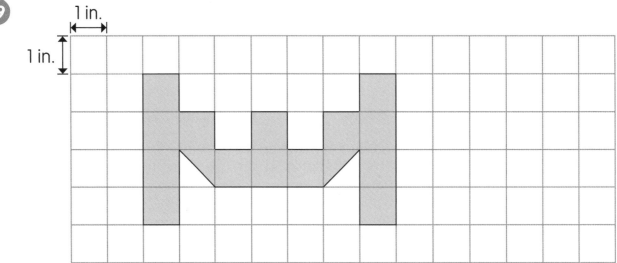

The area of the given figure is _____ square inches.

20

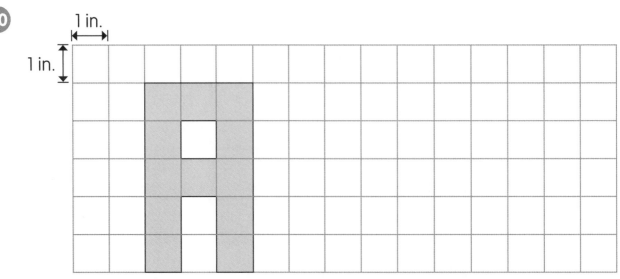

The area of the given figure is _____ square inches.

Name: _____ Date: _____

Activity 3 Square Units (m² and ft²)

**Find the area of each figure in square meters (m²).
Then, answer each question.**

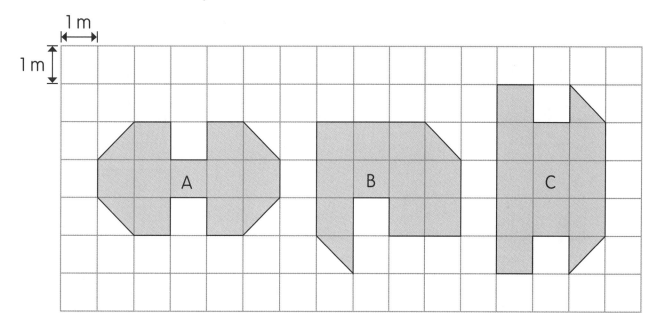

1

Figure	A	B	C
Area			

2 Which figure has the largest area?

Figure _____ has the largest area.

3 Which figures have the same area?

Figures _____ and _____ have the same area.

Match the figures with the same area in square meters (m²).

4

a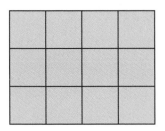

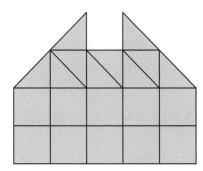

b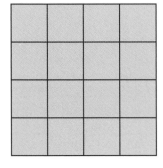

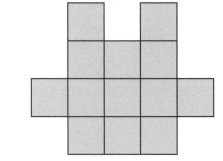

c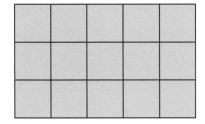

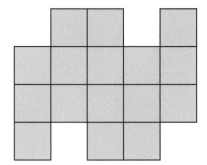

d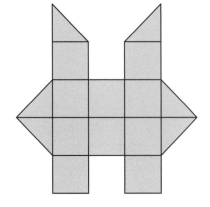

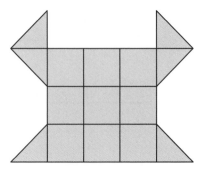

**Find the area of each figure in square feet (ft²).
Then, answer each question.**

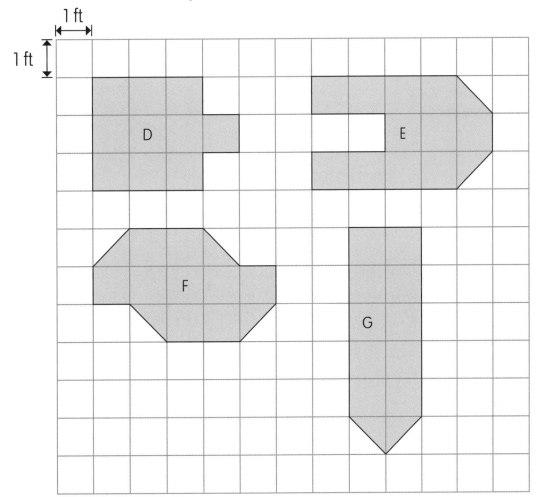

Figure	D	E	F	G
Area				

5

6 Which figure has the smallest area?

Figure _____ has the smallest area.

7 Which figure has the largest area?

Figure _____ has the largest area.

8 Which figures have the same area?

Figures _____ and _____ have the same area.

Match the figures with the same area in square feet (ft²).

9

a
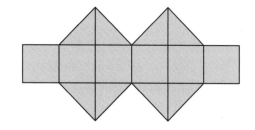

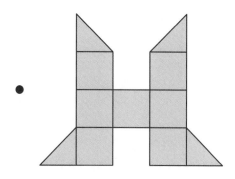

b
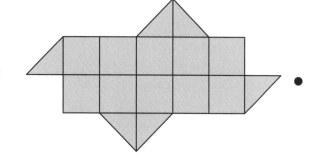

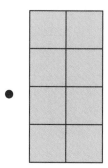

c
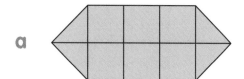

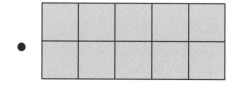

d
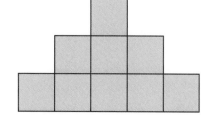

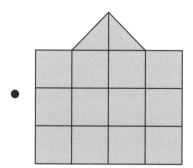

Extra Practice and Homework Grade 3B

Extra Practice and Homework
Area and Perimeter

Chapter 9

Activity 4   Perimeter and Area

Find the area and perimeter of each figure.
Then, answer each question.

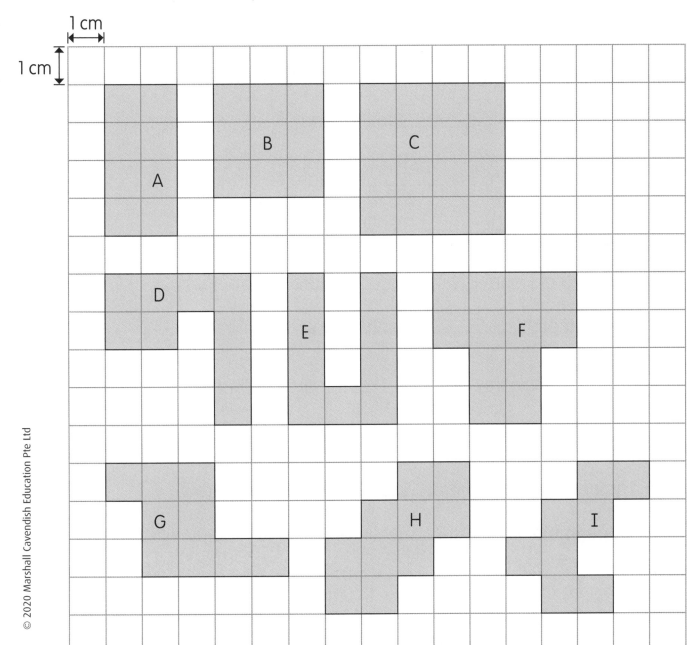

1. The area of Figure A is _____ square centimeters.

   Its perimeter is _____ centimeters.

2. The area of Figure B is _____ square centimeters.

   Its perimeter is _____ centimeters.

3. The area of Figure C is _____ square centimeters.

   Its perimeter is _____ centimeters.

4. The area of Figure D is _____ square centimeters.

   Its perimeter is _____ centimeters.

5. The area of Figure E is _____ square centimeters.

   Its perimeter is _____ centimeters.

6. The area of Figure F is _____ square centimeters.

   Its perimeter is _____ centimeters.

7. The area of Figure G is _____ square centimeters.

   Its perimeter is _____ centimeters.

8. The area of Figure H is _____ square centimeters.

   Its perimeter is _____ centimeters.

9. The area of Figure I is _____ square centimeters.

   Its perimeter is _____ centimeters.

10 Figure _____ has the largest area.

11 Figures _____, _____, and _____ have the same area as Figure _____.

12 Both Figures A and I have the same _____. The area of each figure is _____ square centimeters.

13 Figure _____ has the longest perimeter.

14 Figures _____ and _____ have the shortest perimeter.

15 Figures _____, _____, and _____ have the same perimeter as Figure _____.

Use the grid to draw a figure that has the same area and perimeter as each of the given figures.

16

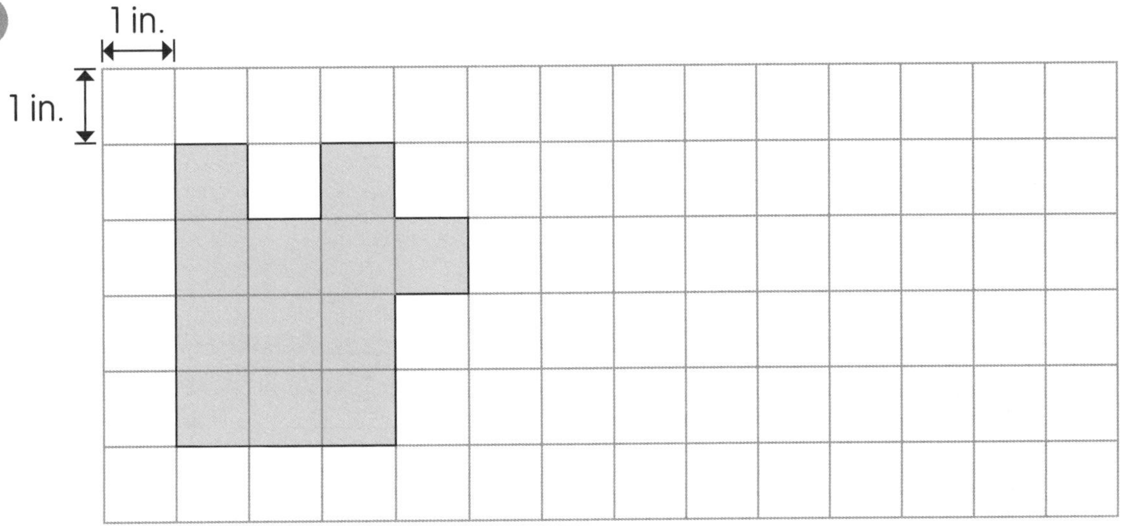

a   The area of the given figure is _____ square inches.

b   The perimeter of the given figure is _____ inches.

17

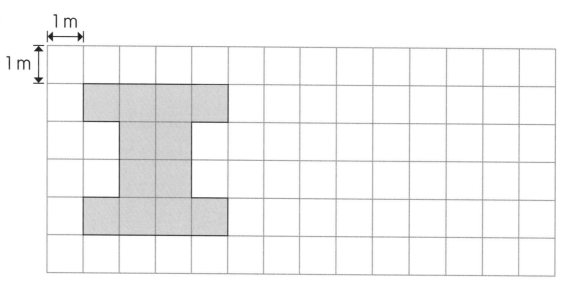

a   The area of the given figure is _____ square meters.

b   The perimeter of the given figure is _____ meters.

18

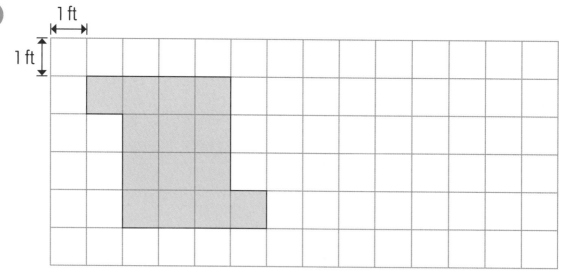

a   The area of the given figure is _____ square feet.

b   The perimeter of the given figure is _____ feet.

Fill in each blank.

19 The figure shows a square handkerchief.
Find the area of the handkerchief.

9 cm

9 cm

Length of the handkerchief = _____ cm

Width of the handkerchief = _____ cm

_____ × _____ = _____

Area of the handkerchief = _____ cm²

20 The figure shows a rectangular plot of land.
Find the area of the plot of land.

8 m

20 m

Length of the plot of land = _____ m

Width of the plot of land = _____ m

_____ × _____ = _____

Area of the plot of land = _____ m²

21 The figure shows a rectangular swimming pool.
Find the area of the swimming pool.

9 m

25 m

Length of the swimming pool = _____ m

Width of the swimming pool = _____ m

_____ × _____ = _____

Area of the swimming pool = _____ m²

Draw lines to separate each figure into rectangles.
Then, find the area of each figure.

22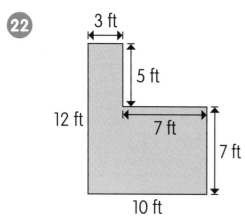

23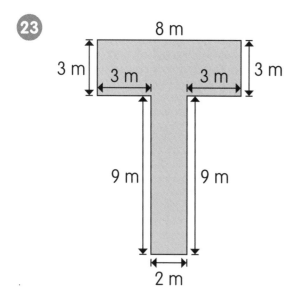

24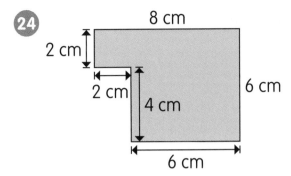
8 cm

2 cm

2 cm

4 cm

6 cm

6 cm

Use the figure to answer each question.

25 The figure shows the shape of Ms. Bennett's vegetable farm. Find the area of Ms. Bennett's vegetable farm.

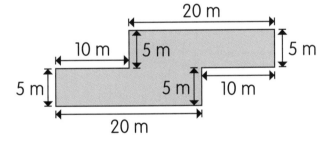
20 m

10 m

5 m

5 m

5 m

10 m

5 m

20 m

26 The figure shows the shape of a field.
    Find the area of the field.

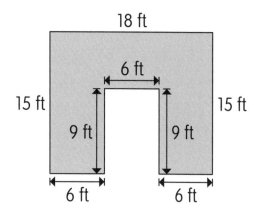

27 The figure shows the floor plan of Matthew's home.
    What is the floor area of Matthew's home?

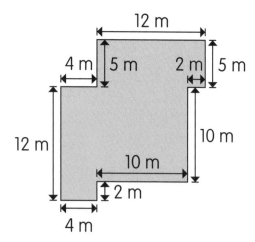

Chapter 9

Extra Practice and Homework
Area and Perimeter

Activity 5   More Perimeter

Find the perimeter of each figure.

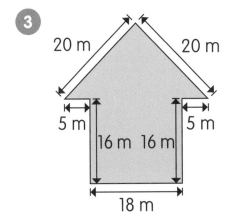

1. 18 ft
    49 ft

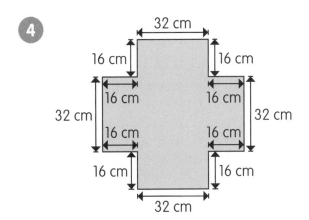

2. 27 in.
    27 in.

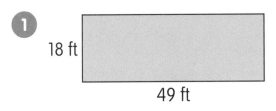

3. 20 m   20 m
    5 m   5 m
    16 m   16 m
    18 m

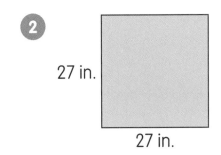

4. 32 cm
    16 cm   16 cm
    16 cm   16 cm
    32 cm   32 cm
    16 cm   16 cm
    16 cm   16 cm
    32 cm

Use a centimeter ruler or inch ruler to measure the sides of each figure. Then, find the perimeter of each figure.

5

Perimeter = _____ in.

6

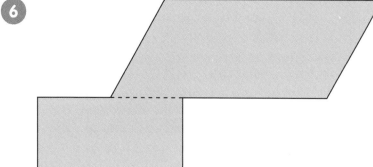

Perimeter = _____ cm

Use the figure to answer each question.

7 Jasmine sticks some ribbon along the edges of a table top.
The length of the table top is 6 feet long.
The width of the table top is 4 feet long.
What is the length of ribbon she needs?

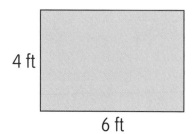

4 ft

6 ft

8 Each side of a square picture frame is 13 centimeters.
A piece of ribbon is placed along the sides of the frame.
What is the length of the ribbon?

9 22 square pots of plants are arranged as shown.
The side of each pot is 1 feet.
What is the area of space framed by the pots?

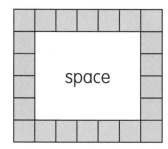

10 The length of a rectangular playground is 3 times its width.
The perimeter of the playground is 96 meters.
Find the length and width of the playground.

length

width

11 The rectangle and the square have the same perimeter.
Find the area of the square.

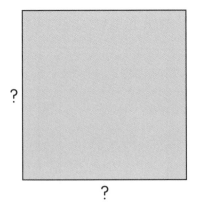

6 cm

12 cm

?

?

Name: _____ Date: _____

Mathematical Habit **4** **Use mathematical models**

Mr. Lee's field has a perimeter of 24 meters.

What could the length and width of his field be? Besides the example shown, draw five other rectangles to show some of the possible answers.

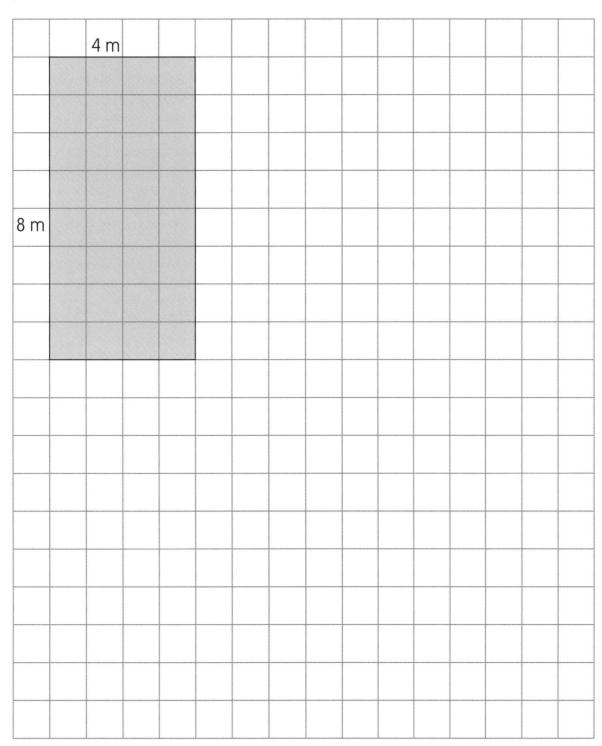

Mathematical Habit 1 Persevere in solving problems

Ms. Scott's garden has two rectangular sections.
She needs to fence up the whole garden to plant some flowers.
What is the total length of fence she needs to put up around the whole garden?

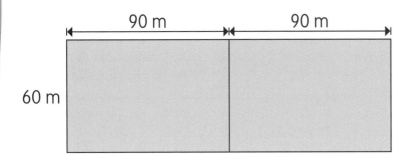

SCHOOL-to-HOME
CONNECTIONS

Chapter 10

Time

Dear Family,

In this chapter, your child will learn about time. Skills your child will practice include:
- telling time to the minute
- using the terms *past* and *to* to tell time
- converting hours and minutes to minutes and vice versa
- finding end time, start time, or elapsed time
- solving real-world problems involving time

Math Practice

There are numerous real-life opportunities for your child to work with time. At the end of this chapter, you may want to carry out this activity with your child. This activity will help to strengthen your child's understanding of time.

Activity

- Ask your child to list all of the things he or she does in a typical school day, starting from when he or she wakes up and continuing through the day until he or she goes to bed. For example, your child might list: brushing teeth, having breakfast, riding the school bus to school, participating in different classes, playing at recess, having lunch, riding the school bus home, doing chores, doing homework, playing, and getting ready for bed.
- Next, encourage your child to think about how much time he or she spends doing each activity. Then, help your child create a timeline marked in hours and half hours.
- Have your child add the day's activities to the timeline, calculating how much time is spent on each activity.
- Use the timeline to ask questions such as, "How much more time do you spend in music class than at lunch? How much time do you spend in all on the school bus each day?"

Math Talk

Help your child understand that **hour (h)** and **minute (min)** are units of measurement used to measure time and that
1 h = 60 min.
Write a time and ask your child to read it. For example,
9:20 is 20 minutes **past** 9.
9:45 is 15 minutes **to** 10.

Help your child understand that a **timeline** is used to find elapsed time, which is the amount of time that has passed between the start and the end of an activity.
For example:

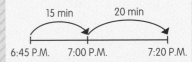

Ask your child when the activity occurs in the day and how he or she knows (the timeline shows that the activity occurs after noon and before midnight, as the times are written using P.M.).

© 2020 Marshall Cavendish Education Pte Ltd

BLANK

Name: _____ Date: _____

Chapter 10 Extra Practice and Homework
Time

Activity 1 Telling Time

Write the time on each clock using "past" or "to."

1

_____

2

_____

3

_____

4

_____

5

_____

6

_____

7

_____

8

_____

9

_____

10

_____

Fill in each blank with the correct time.

11 18 minutes past 2 is _____.

12 13 minutes to 1 is _____.

Find each missing number.

13 8:28 A.M. is _____ minutes past _____ in the morning.

14 6:53 P.M. is _____ minutes to _____ in the evening.

What time is it?

15

The clock is 5 minutes slow.

What is the actual time? _____

Name: _____ Date: _____

Chapter 10 — Extra Practice and Homework Time

Activity 2 Converting Hours and Minutes

Fill in each blank.

1. Ana takes a nap for 2 hours.
How many minutes are there in 2 hours?

   2 hours = _____ minutes

   There are _____ minutes in 2 hours.

2. Daniel watches a movie for 2 hours 15 minutes.
How many minutes are there in 2 hours 15 minutes?

   2 hours 15 minutes = _____ minutes

   There are _____ minutes in 2 hours 15 minutes.

3. A runner takes 67 minutes to complete 10 kilometers.
How many hours and minutes are there in 67 minutes?

   67 minutes = _____ hour _____ minutes

   There are _____ hour _____ minutes in 67 minutes.

4. Brandon takes 103 minutes to do his homework.
How many hours and minutes are there in 103 minutes?

   103 minutes = _____ hour _____ minutes

   There are _____ hour _____ minutes in 103 minutes.

© 2020 Marshall Cavendish Education Pte Ltd

Write each time in minutes.

⑤ 1 h 20 min = _____ min + _____ min

= _____ min

⑥ 2 h 48 min = _____ min + _____ min

= _____ min

⑦ 1 h 40 min = _____ min

⑧ 2 h 25 min = _____ min

⑨ 3 h 59 min = _____ min

⑩ 3 h 37 min = _____ min

> 1 h = 60 min
> 2 h = 120 min
> 3 h = 180 min

Write each time in hours and minutes.

⑪ 135 min = _____ h _____ min

⑫ 187 min = _____ h _____ min

Answer each question.

⑬ Ashanti says that 105 minutes is 1 hour 5 minutes. Is this correct? Explain.

_____

_____

⑭ What is the shortest possible time needed to cook a hard-boiled egg?

| 1 min | 10 min | 30 min | 1 h |

_____

Extra Practice and Homework
Time

Activity 3   Measuring Elapsed Time

Find the elapsed time. Then, fill in each blank.

1   How many hours are there from 2:15 P.M. to 4:15 P.M.?

_____

2   How many hours are there from 9:31 P.M. to 1:31 A.M.?

_____

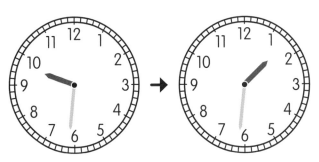

3   How many minutes are there from 7:45 P.M. to 8:15 P.M.?

_____

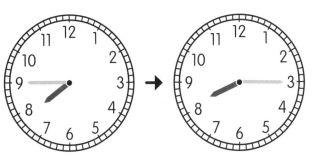

4 How many minutes are there from 11:30 P.M.

to 12:19 A.M.? _____

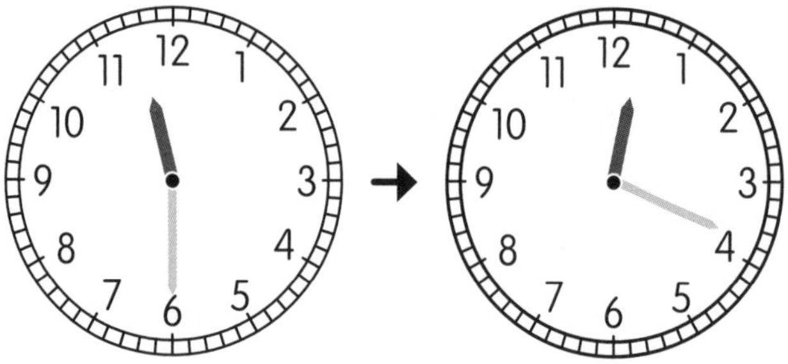

5 How many hours and minutes are there from 7:53 A.M.

to 10:46 A.M.? _____

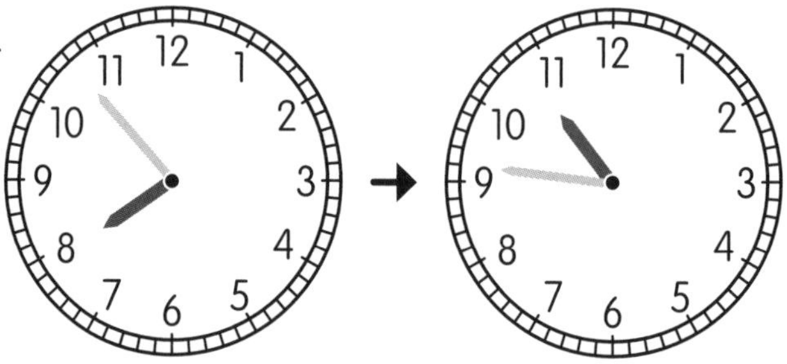

6 How many hours and minutes are there from 11:12 A.M.

to 3:27 P.M.? _____

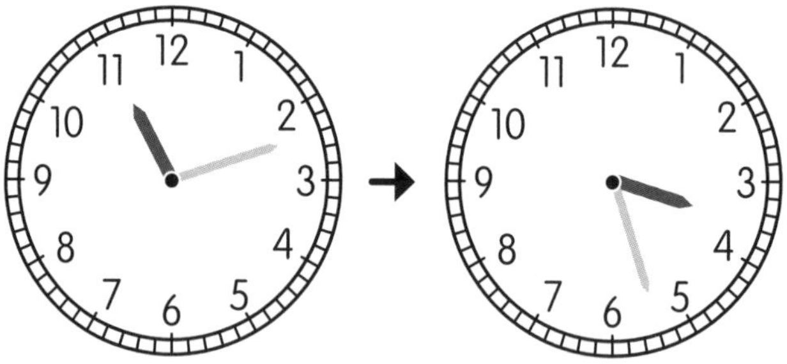

7 How many hours and minutes are there from 10:04 A.M.

to 2:41 P.M.? _____

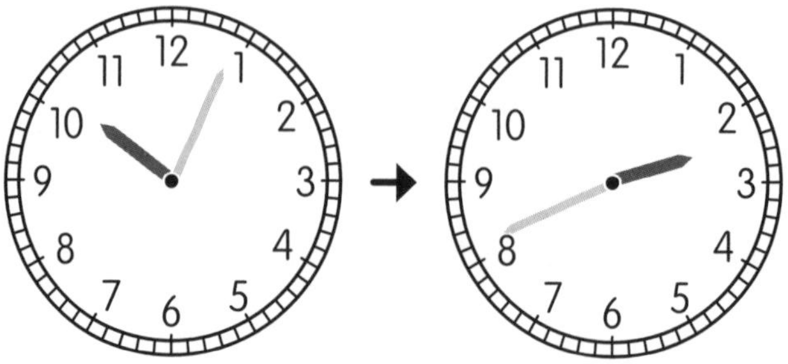

Fill in each blank.

8 What time is

a 2 hours after 8:00 P.M.? _____

b 30 minutes after 1:36 P.M.? _____

c 3 hours after 10:25 A.M.? _____

d 4 hours after 12:00 P.M.? _____

e 6 hours after 6:03 A.M.? _____

f 15 minutes after 9:24 A.M.? _____

g 25 minutes after 7:07 A.M.? _____

h 37 minutes after 11:48 A.M.? _____

i 3 hours before 6:40 A.M.? _____

j 45 minutes before 7:08 A.M.? _____

k 2 hours before 1:20 P.M.? _____

l 2 hours before 8:30 P.M.? _____

m 49 minutes before 4:45 A.M.? _____

n 40 minutes before 8:30 A.M.? _____

o 53 minutes before 2:19 P.M.? _____

p 1 hour 15 minutes before 3:33 A.M.? _____

Solve. Show your work. Draw a timeline to help you.

9 Alex was at his friend's house from 11:50 A.M. to 3.15 P.M.
How long was his visit?

10 Daniela started reading a book at 2:35 P.M.
She took 3 hours 10 minutes to finish reading the book.
At what time did she finish reading the book?

11 Lily went to the library.
She was there for 2 hours 15 minutes.
She left the library at 5:40 P.M.
At what time did she reach the library?

12 María spent 50 minutes practising karate.
Then, she spent 2 hours 15 minutes doing her homework.
How long did she spend on the two tasks?

13 Ms. Turner took 1 hour 10 minutes to sew a dress.
    Riley took 2 hours 40 minutes to sew a similar dress.
    How much longer did Riley take to sew the dress than Ms. Turner?

14 Ryan took 50 minutes to bake a cake.
    How long did he take to bake 4 similar cakes?
    Give your answer in hours and minutes.

15 Mr. Smith left home at 6:35 A.M.
He took 1 hour 5 minutes to travel to his office.
At what time did he reach his office?

16 Kayla spends 5 hours 30 minutes in school.
She reaches school at 7:25 A.M.
At what time does she leave school?

17 Mr. Cox sewed two blouses.
He took 3 hours 40 minutes to sew the first blouse and
2 hours 55 minutes to sew the second blouse.
He finished sewing the blouses at 8:10 P.M.
At what time did he start sewing?

18 Bella left home at 6:15 A.M.
She took 1 hour 55 minutes to cycle to a nearby park and
2 hours 20 minutes to cycle home.

   a   How long did she spend cycling in all?

   b   At what time did she return home?

19 Mr. Evans finished his work at 5:10 P.M. according to his watch. His watch was 15 minutes slow.

a   What was the actual time he finished work?

b   He worked for 8 hours 15 minutes.
      What was the actual time he started work?

20 Mr. Jones drove from his office to a restaurant.
He took 1 hour 45 minutes to reach the restaurant as there was a traffic jam.

a   He left his office at 6:20 P.M.
    At what time did he reach the restaurant?

b   If there was no traffic jam, he would have reached the restaurant at 7:35 P.M. How long more did he take with the jam?

21 Carla flew to Hong Kong.
The flight took 14 hours 6 minutes.

    a   The plane took off at 7:45 A.M.
         At what time did she arrive in Hong Kong?

    b   Sara took another flight which took 15 minutes longer than
         the flight Carla took.
         How long was Sara's flight?

22 Zoey ran round a track.
She completed one round in 15 minutes.

a How long did she take to run 3 rounds?

b Zoey started running at 7:30 A.M.
At what time did she finish running 3 rounds?

Extra Practice and Homework Grade 3B

3 Measuring Elapsed Time **97**

© 2020 Marshall Cavendish Education Pte Ltd

23 Madison made 3 bangles.
She took 3 hours to make each bangle.

    a   How long did she take to make 3 bangles?

    b   She started making them at 11:00 A.M.
        At what time did she finish?

24 Mr. Lee had an interview arranged for 3:20 P.M.
He arrived at the company 35 minutes before the arranged time.
However, his interview was pushed back to 3:35 P.M.
How long did he have to wait to be interviewed?

25 Ms. Lopez had an interview arranged for 1.40 P.M.
She arrived at the location 5 minutes late.
Luckily, her interview was postponed to 1.55 P.M.
How long did she have to wait to be interviewed?

Name: _____ Date: _____

1 **Mathematical Habit 4** **Use mathematical models**

Blake wanted to find out how much time Hayden took to make a kite.

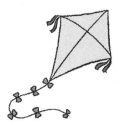

Hayden started at 2:20 P.M. and ended at 5:05 P.M.
Blake drew this timeline to help him find the duration:

2:20 P.M.   5:05 P.M.

How can you improve the timeline?

2 **Mathematical Habit 2** **Use mathematical reasoning**

Write in hours and minutes.
Draw or explain the steps you take to get the answer.

135 min = _____ h _____ min

Mathematical Habit 4 **Use mathematical models**

Diego fell ill and visited a doctor.
The doctor gave him some tablets and told him to take them every 4 hours.
He took his first tablet for the day at 9:30 A.M.
At what time should he take his fourth tablet?

SCHOOL-to-HOME
CONNECTIONS

Chapter 11

Graphs and Line Plots

Dear Family,

In this chapter, your child will learn to make picture graphs, bar graphs, and line plots, and interpret the data presented in them. Skills your child will practice include:

- making and interpreting picture graphs with scales
- making and interpreting bar graphs with scales
- using a ruler to estimate and measure given lengths to the nearest quarter, half, or whole inch
- showing data on a line plot where the horizontal scale is marked off in whole numbers, halves, or quarters

Math Practice

Graphs and line plots are useful for recording and presenting information, or data, collected in surveys. At the end of this chapter, you may want to carry out these activities with your child. These activities will help your child practice collecting and presenting data.

Activity 1

- Have your child pick a topic, such as, a favorite color. Then, have your child survey family members and friends to learn their favorite choice within the topic.
- Help your child present the data in a picture or bar graph. Your child may want to draw a picture or bar graph, or use a digital tool to create it.
- Ask your child to explain the bar graph's features and interpret the data it represents. To prompt discussion, ask questions such as, "Which color do people like most? How many more people like green than yellow?"

Math Talk

Ask your child to talk about and show examples of the different kinds of picture graphs, bar graphs, and line plots found in his or her math book.

Ask your child to explain the **scale** on a bar graph, meaning the distance between two markings on the graph.

Then, ask your child to explain the purpose of a **survey,** which is a method of collecting information, or data. Ask your child to recall an experience such as watching a television advertisement that mentions surveys of people's preferences. Encourage your child to explain what he or she learned from the survey.

Activity 2

- Prepare a line plot with the horizontal scale marked off in $\frac{1}{4}$ in., $\frac{1}{2}$ in., $\frac{3}{4}$ in., 1 in., $1\frac{1}{4}$ in., $1\frac{1}{2}$ in., $1\frac{3}{4}$ in., and 2 in. as shown.

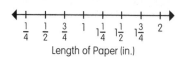

Length of Paper (in.)

- Cut out strips of paper of length $\frac{1}{4}$ in., $\frac{1}{2}$ in., $\frac{3}{4}$ in., 1 in., $1\frac{1}{4}$ in., $1\frac{1}{2}$ in., $1\frac{3}{4}$ in., and 2 in. (prepare different numbers of each length). Put all the strips of paper into a bag.
- Have your child pick one strip of paper.
- Ask your child to measure the length of the strip of paper and mark (✗) the result on the line plot.
- Repeat until the bag is empty. Then, discuss the results together.

Chapter 11 Extra Practice and Homework
Graphs and Line Plots

Activity 1 Making Picture Graphs with Scales

Ms. Murphy bought 4 different flavors of bagels for her class.

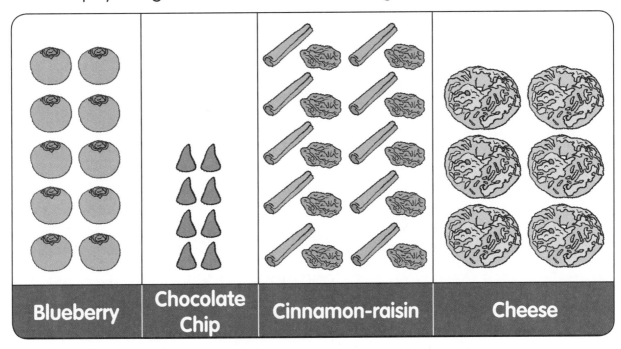

| Blueberry | Chocolate Chip | Cinnamon-raisin | Cheese |

Use the data to complete the table.

1	Flavor	Tally	Number
	Blueberry	卌 卌	
	Chocolate Chip	卌 |||	8
	Cinnamon-raisin	卌 卌	
	Cheese	卌		

Use the data in the table in question ① to complete the picture graph.

② **Number of Different Flavored Bagels**

| Blueberry | Chocolate Chip | Cinnamon-raisin | Cheese |

Key: Each ● stands for 2 bagels.

Use the data in the picture graph to answer each question.

③ Ms. Murphy bought _____ bagels.

④ Ms. Murphy bought _____ cinnamon-raisin bagels.

⑤ Ms. Murphy bought an equal number of _____ and _____ bagels.

⑥ Ms. Murphy bought _____ more cinnamon-raisin bagels than cheese bagels.

Some students visited Thailand, Vietnam, Laos, Australia, and New Zealand during their vacation.

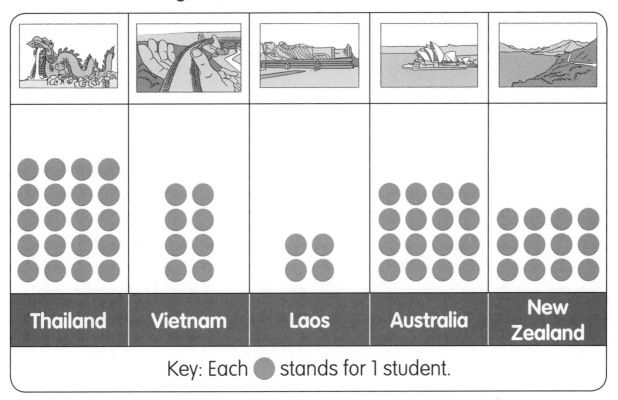

Key: Each ⬤ stands for 1 student.

Use the data to complete the table.

7

Country	Tally	Number of Students
Thailand	✙✙✙ ✙✙✙ ✙✙✙ ✙✙✙	
Vietnam		8
Laos		
Australia		
New Zealand		

Use the data in the table to complete the picture graph.

8　**Number of Students who had Visited the Five Countries**

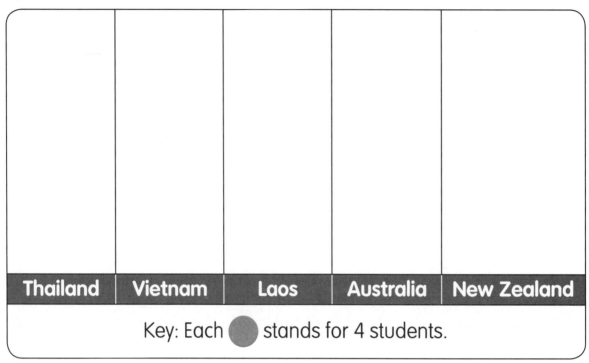

| Thailand | Vietnam | Laos | Australia | New Zealand |

Key: Each ● stands for 4 students.

Use the data in the picture graph to answer each question.

9　_____ students visited Vietnam.

10　_____ students visited Australia.

11　The greatest number of students visited _____.

12　The least number of students visited _____.

13　4 fewer students visited _____ than _____.

14　8 more students visited _____ than _____.

15　The number of students who visited _____ is more than
the number of students who visited Laos but fewer than
the number of students who visited Australia.

Extra Practice and Homework
Graphs and Line Plots

Activity 2   Making Bar Graphs with Scales

Mr. Anderson conducted a survey to find out the favorite fruit of some children. He recorded the children's favorite fruit in a tally chart.

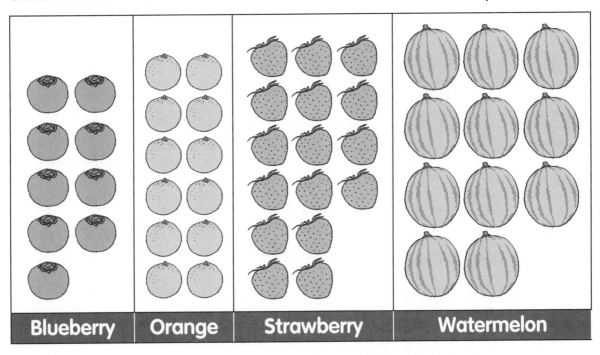

| Blueberry | Orange | Strawberry | Watermelon |

Complete the tally chart.

1

Children's Favorite Fruit

Kinds of Fruit	Tally	Number of Fruit
Blueberry	⅏ ⅲ	
Orange	⅏ ⅏ ⅱ	
Strawberry	⅏ ⅏ ⅏ ⅰ	
Watermelon	⅏ ⅏ ⅰ	

Use the data in the tally chart to complete the bar graph.

2

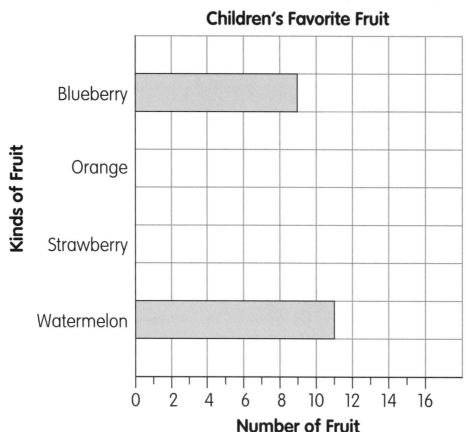

Children's Favorite Fruit

Use the bar graph to answer each question.

3 The scale shows skip counts of _____.

4 _____ children like blueberries.

5 _____ children like strawberries.

6 Most children like _____.

7 The least number of children like _____.

The picture graph shows the number of cars in a parking lot.

Number of Different Colored Cars in a Parking Lot

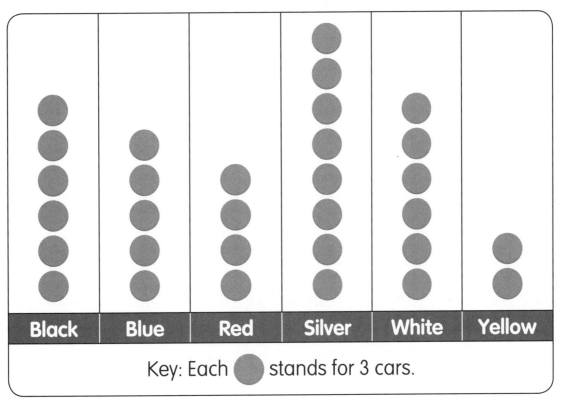

Key: Each ⬤ stands for 3 cars.

Use the picture graph to complete the bar graph.

8

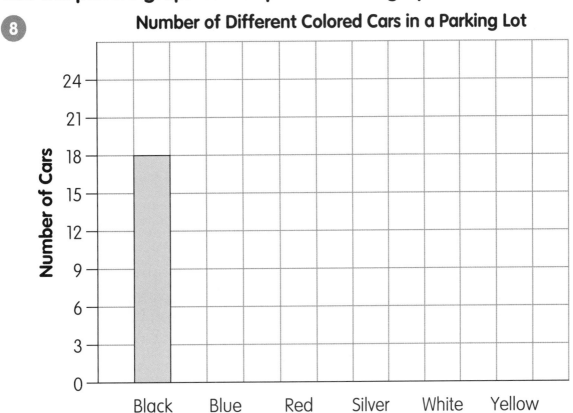

Use the bar graph in question 8 to answer each question.

9 The scale shows skip counts of _____.

10 There are _____ red cars in the parking lot.

11 There are _____ silver cars in the parking lot.

12 The parking lot has the least number of _____ cars.

13 The parking lot has the greatest number of _____ cars.

The picture graph shows the different flavors of cups of jelly Ms. Miller made for a party.

Different Flavors of Cups of Jelly

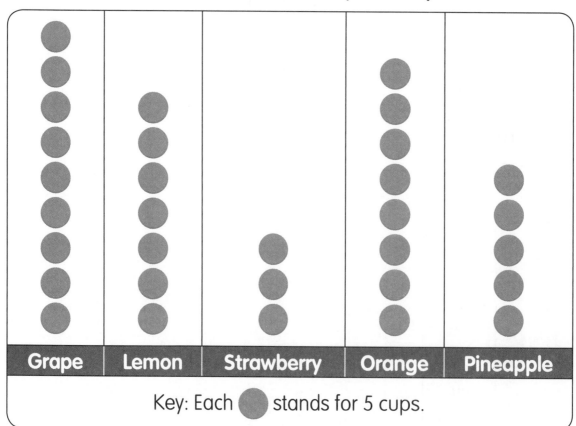

Key: Each ⬤ stands for 5 cups.

Extra Practice and Homework Grade 3B

Use the picture graph on the previous page to complete the bar graph.

14

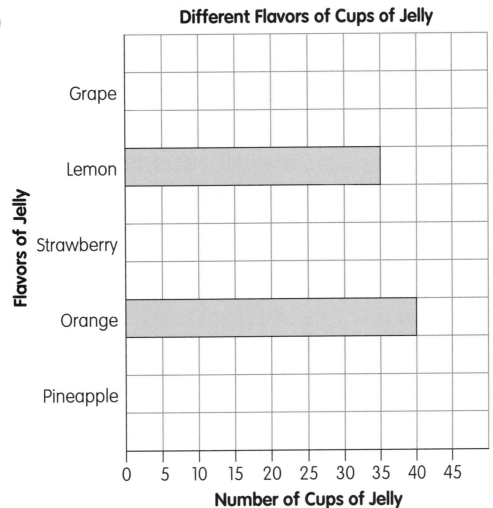

Different Flavors of Cups of Jelly

Flavors of Jelly

Grape

Lemon

Strawberry

Orange

Pineapple

0   5   10   15   20   25   30   35   40   45

Number of Cups of Jelly

Use the bar graph to answer each question.

15 The scale shows skip counts of _____.

16 Ms. Miller made _____ cups of lemon jelly.

17 Ms. Miller made _____ cups of orange jelly.

18 The most popular flavor is the _____ jelly.

A survey was carried out to find the hair colors of some third graders. It was found that …

8 students have brown hair.

12 students have blond hair.

3 times as many students have black hair as brown hair.

2 fewer students have auburn hair than brown hair.

Complete the bar graph. Then, fill in the missing hair colors.

19

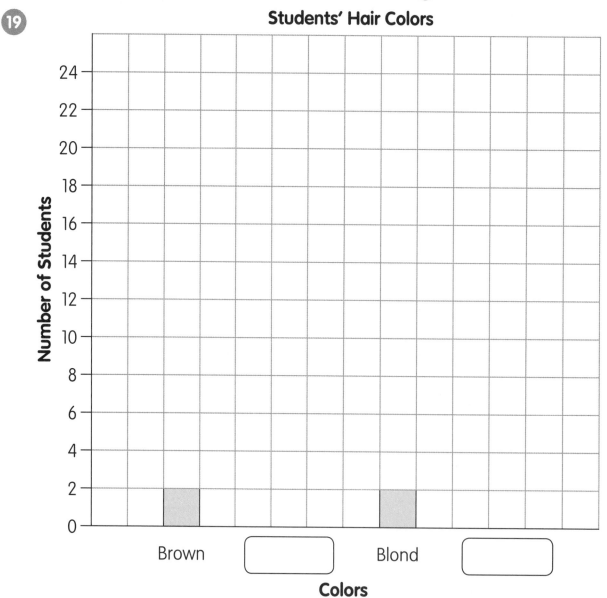

Students' Hair Colors

Chapter 11

Extra Practice and Homework
Graphs and Line Plots

Activity 3 Reading and Interpreting Bar Graphs

Use the data in the bar graph to answer each question.

The bar graph shows the kinds of toys that a store has.

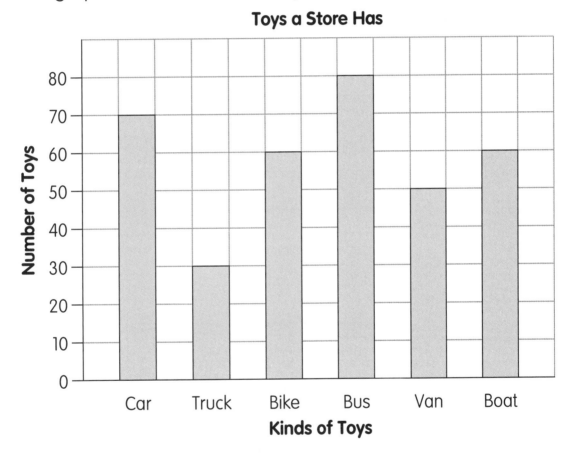

Toys a Store Has

1. The scale shows skip counts of _____.

2. The store has _____ cars.

3. The store has _____ vans.

4. The store has the least number of _____.

5 The store has the most number of _____.

6 There are 40 more _____ than _____.

7 There are 30 fewer _____ than _____.

8 There is an equal number of _____ and _____.

9 The store has _____ toys altogether.

Use the data in the bar graph to answer each question.

The bar graph shows the different shapes of the blocks in a box.

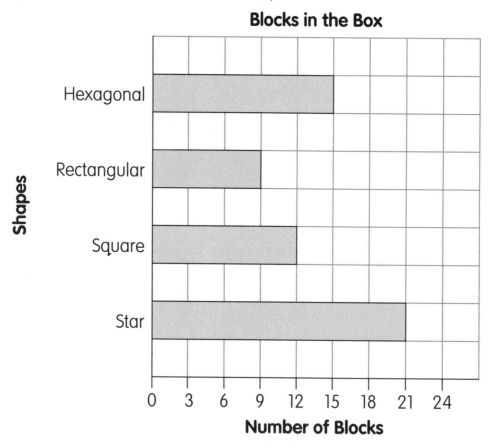

Blocks in the Box

10 The scale shows skip counts of _____.

11 The box has the least number of _____ blocks.

12 The box has the greatest number of _____ blocks.

13 There are _____ more hexagonal than square blocks.

14 There is a total of _____ rectangular and star blocks.

15 There are _____ blocks altogether.

Use the data in the bar graph to answer each question.

The bar graph shows the number of different types of trees a plant nursery sells over six months.

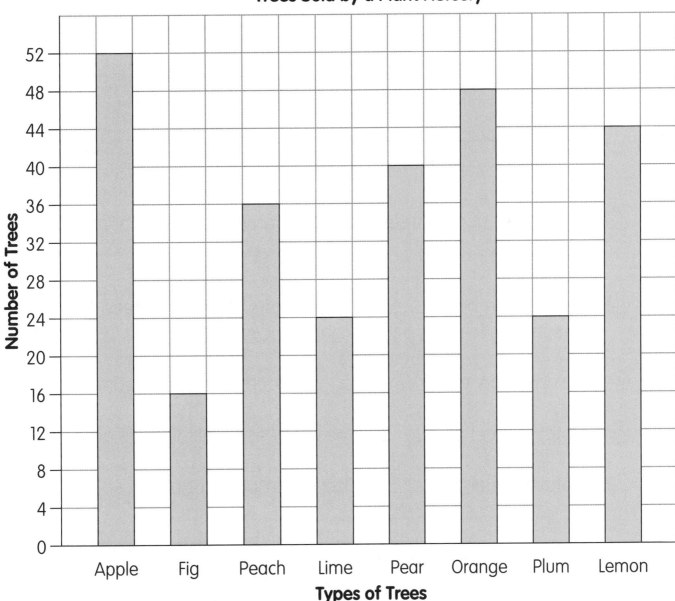

Trees Sold by a Plant Nursery

16 The scale shows skip counts of _____.

17 The greatest number of _____ trees are sold.

18 The least number of _____ trees are sold.

19 20 more _____ trees than _____ trees are sold.

20 16 fewer _____ trees than _____ trees are sold.

21 8 fewer _____ trees than _____ trees are sold.

22 4 more _____ trees than _____ trees are sold.

23 The total number of _____ trees and _____ trees sold is the same as the number of apple trees sold.

24 The number of pear trees sold is the same as the total number of _____ trees and _____ trees sold.

25 The total number of _____ trees and _____ trees sold is the same as the number of orange trees sold.

26 A total number of 100 _____ trees and _____ trees are sold.

27 A total number of _____ peach trees and lime trees are sold.

28 A total number of _____ trees are sold altogether.

© 2020 Marshall Cavendish Education Pte Ltd

Chapter 11
Extra Practice and Homework
Graphs and Line Plots

Activity 4   Line Plots and Estimation

Estimate the length of each line segment without using a ruler. Then, measure each line segment to the nearest quarter inch.

1 •————————————————• Line segment A

Estimated length: _____ in.

Measured length: _____ in.

2 •—————————————————• Line segment B

Estimated length: _____ in.

Measured length: _____ in.

3 •————• Line segment C

Estimated length: _____ in.

Measured length: _____ in.

4 •——————————• Line segment D

Estimated length: _____ in.

Measured length: _____ in.

Use the line segments in questions ① to ④ to check (✔) each correct statement.

5 Line segment A is more than $2\frac{3}{4}$ inches but less than 3 inches long. ☐

6 Line segment A is 2 inches to the nearest half inch. ☐

7 Line segment A is $2\frac{3}{4}$ inches to the nearest quarter inch. ☐

8 Line segment B is more than $3\frac{1}{2}$ inches but less than 4 inches long. ☐

9 Line segment B is 4 inches to the nearest half inch. ☐

10 Line segment B is $3\frac{1}{2}$ inches to the nearest quarter inch. ☐

11 Line segment C is more than 1 inch but less than $1\frac{1}{2}$ inches long. ☐

12 Line segment C is 1 inch to the nearest half inch. ☐

13 Line segment C is $1\frac{3}{4}$ inches to the nearest quarter inch. ☐

14 Line segment D is more than $2\frac{1}{2}$ inches but less than 3 inches long. ☐

15 Line segment D is 2 inches to the nearest half inch. ☐

16 Line segment D is $2\frac{1}{4}$ inches to the nearest quarter inch. ☐

© 2020 Marshall Cavendish Education Pte Ltd

Measure the length of each leaf.
Then, check (✔) each correct statement.

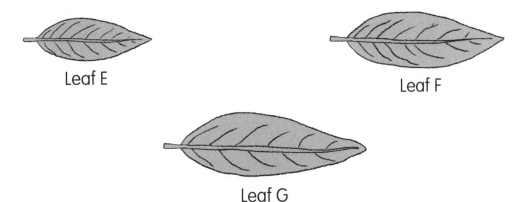

Leaf E

Leaf F

Leaf G

17 Leaf E is more than $1\frac{1}{2}$ inches but less than 2 inches long. ☐

18 Leaf F is 2 inches to the nearest half inch. ☐

19 Leaf G is $2\frac{1}{4}$ inches to the nearest quarter inch. ☐

20 Leaf E is $1\frac{1}{4}$ inches to the nearest inches. ☐

21 Leaf F is $1\frac{3}{4}$ inches to the nearest quarter inch. ☐

22 Leaf G is 2 inches to the nearest half inch. ☐

23 Leaf E is more than $1\frac{1}{4}$ inches but less than $1\frac{3}{4}$ inches long. ☐

24 Leaf F is 1 inch to the nearest inches. ☐

25 Leaf G is $2\frac{1}{2}$ inches to the nearest quarter inch. ☐

Study the given data carefully.
Then, show your data on the line plot.

26 **a** There are 25 children in all.

    b None of the children have a height of 41 inches, $42\frac{1}{2}$ inches, and $44\frac{1}{2}$ inches.

    c One child has a height of 40 inches and another child has a height of $43\frac{1}{2}$ inches.

    d Two children have a height of $40\frac{1}{2}$ inches, 42 inches, and 45 inches each.

    e There are twice as many children with a height of 43 inches and $45\frac{1}{2}$ inches each, as those with a height of $40\frac{1}{2}$ inches.

    f The number of children with a height of $41\frac{1}{2}$ inches is one more than those with a height of 45 inches.

    g The greatest number of children have a height of 44 inches.

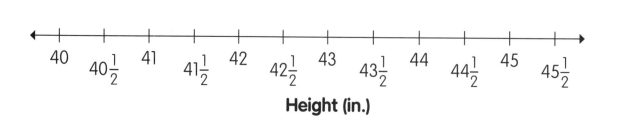

Height (in.)

Mathematical Habit 1 Persevere in solving problems

Number the steps for creating a line plot.

Number	Step
	Check out your data and see what the largest and smallest data is. 0 1 2 3 4 5 6 7 8
	Organize your data in numerical order from the smallest to the largest. Students | No. of books read Student 1 | 5 Student 2 | 1 Student 3 | 2 Student 4 | 5 Student 5 | 8 Student 6 | 0 Student 7 | 3 Student 8 | 2 Student 9 | 2 Student 10 | 1 0 1 1 2 2 2 3 5 5 8
	Mark an ✗ above the horizontal line every time the data occurs. 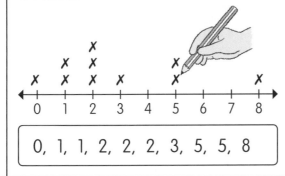 0, 1, 1, 2, 2, 2, 3, 5, 5, 8

MATH JOURNAL

Interpret the data in a line plot.

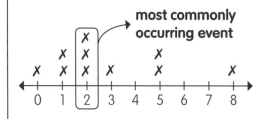

Gather your data, which comprises the rate with which a certain act or event occurs within a given set of people or things.

Students	No. of books read
Student 1	5
Student 2	1
Student 3	2
Student 4	5
Student 5	8
Student 6	0
Student 7	3
Student 8	2
Student 9	2
Student 10	1

Mathematical Habit 2 Use mathematical reasoning

STEP 1 Roll two dice and add the numbers rolled.

STEP 2 Keep a tally of the number of times a sum is obtained. Record these numbers in the tally chart.

STEP 3 Repeat STEP 1 and STEP 2 for a total of 30 rolls.

Sum of the Numbers Rolled	Number of Times	Tally
2		
3		
4		
5		
6		
7		
8		
9		
10		
11		
12		

Use the data in the table to complete the line plot.

a

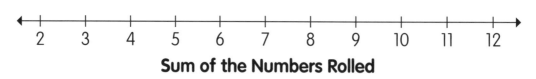

Sum of the Numbers Rolled

b   Is it easy to get a 12? Explain.

_____

_____

c   Which number is the easiest to get? Explain.

_____

_____

SCHOOL-to-HOME
CONNECTIONS

Chapter 12

Angles, Lines, and Two-Dimensional Figures

Dear Family,

In this chapter, your child will learn about angles, lines, and two-dimensional, or flat, shapes. Skills your child will practice include:

- finding angles in plane figures and real-world objects
- comparing angles to a right angle
- defining and identifying perpendicular and parallel lines
- identifying open and closed plane figures, special polygons, and special quadrilaterals
- recognizing polygons by their attributes

Math Practice

We are surrounded by angles, lines, and two-dimensional shapes. With your child, look for examples in your home, such as the parallel lines formed by window blinds, the perpendicular lines that form right angles on door corners, and the surfaces of objects like the table tops, cupboard doors, window frames, television sets, and kites. At the end of this chapter, you may want to carry out these activities with your child. These activities will help to strengthen your child's understanding of angles, parallel lines, perpendicular lines, and help your child identify polygons.

Activity 1

- Help your child fold a rectangular piece of paper to make a variety of angles to identify. Use the folded piece of paper to reinforce acute or obtuse angles to your child.

Activity 2

- Take your child outdoors to locate more parallel and perpendicular line segments, as well as angles. For example, the parallel line segments formed along crosswalks, and the perpendicular line segments that form right angles at the corners of square and rectangular street and park signs.

Explain to your child that when two line segments share the same endpoint, they form an **angle**.

Angle *a* is a **right angle**.

Help your child see that **perpendicular lines** are at right angles to each other.

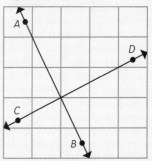

Parallel lines will never meet, even if they are extended.

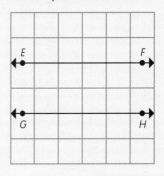

Activity 3
- Look at online images of common road signs, such as:
  - a yield sign (triangle)
  - a street name or speed limit sign (rectangle)
  - a sign alerting drivers to an upcoming traffic signal or to road crews working (rhombus)
  - a stop sign (octagon)

Activity 4
- Check out a book at your local library or go online to find examples of origami, or paper folding.
- To make an origami animal, have your child use a ruler to measure and cut a square from a piece of notebook paper.
- Then, help him or her follow the directions for creating an animal, discussing the kinds of polygons they can identify from the folds.

 Math Talk

Explain to your child that a **polygon** is a closed figure formed by three or more line segments.

Use the following **pentagon** to help your child recognize that the prefix *penta* means "5." Have your child identify the 5 **sides,** 5 **vertices** (the plural form of *vertex*, the point at which two lines or line segments meet), and 5 **angles**.

Next, use the following **rhombus** to help your child recognize that the prefix *quad* means "4." Point out that a **quadrilateral** is a polygon with 4 sides, 4 vertices, and 4 angles.

Then, ask your child to identify two pairs of **parallel lines** in the rhombus.

Chapter 12 Extra Practice and Homework
Angles, Lines, and Two-Dimensional Figures

Activity 1 Introducing Angles

Identify each figure as a point, line, or line segment.

1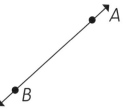

A

B

_____

2 Y

X

_____

3

P

Q

_____

4

T

_____

Check (✔) the statements that are true.

5 A line segment is part of a line.

☐

6 A point is an exact location in space.

☐

7 A line has two endpoints.

☐

Check (✔) the box if an angle is shown. Then, mark the angle.

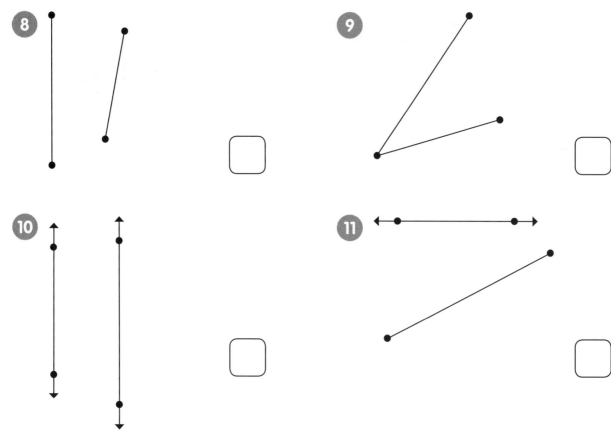

8 □

9 □

10 □

11 □

12 □

13 □

Mark two angles on each object.

14

15

Extra Practice and Homework Grade 3B

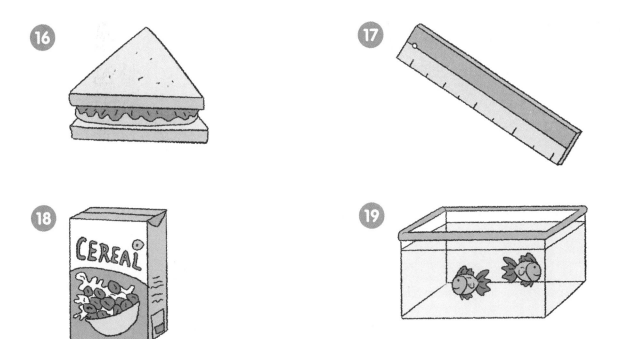

Mark two angles in each flat shape if possible.

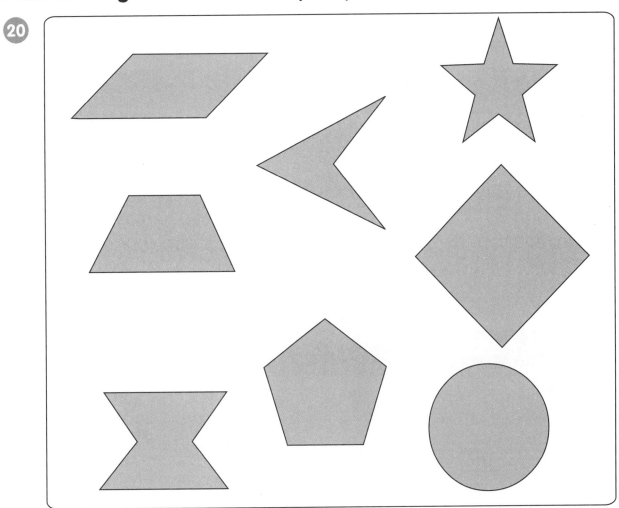

Fill in each blank.

Compare the angles. Use a piece of folded paper ⌐ to help you.

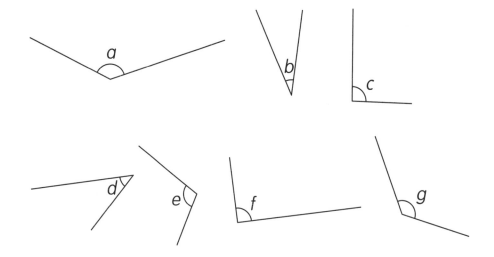

(21) Which of these angles are less than right angles? _____

(22) Which of these angles are greater than right angles? _____

(23) Which of these angles are right angles? _____

Solve.

Where can you find angles less than a right angle, angles greater than a right angle, and right angles in the objects around your class? Record your findings in a table.

		Objects		
(24)	**Angles Less Than a Right Angle**			
(25)	**Angles Greater Than a Right Angle**			
(26)	**Right Angles**			

Extra Practice and Homework Grade 3B

Chapter 12

Extra Practice and Homework
Angles, Lines, and Two-Dimensional Figures

Activity 2   Introducing Perpendicular and Parallel Lines

Use a colored pencil to trace a pair of perpendicular lines on each object.

1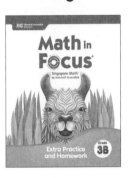

2

3

4

5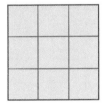

6

Check (✔) the box if the lines are perpendicular.
Trace the pairs of perpendicular lines with a colored pencil and mark ⅃.

7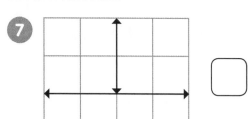

8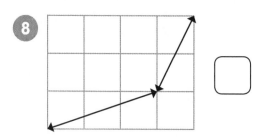

9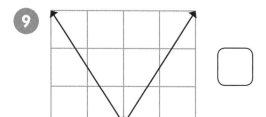

10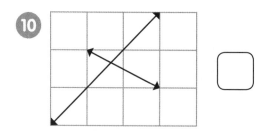

11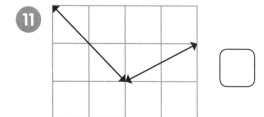

12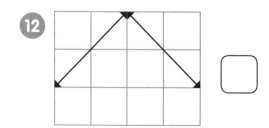

Trace the pairs of perpendicular lines with a colored pencil and mark ⌐. Circle the letters and numbers that have perpendicular lines.

13

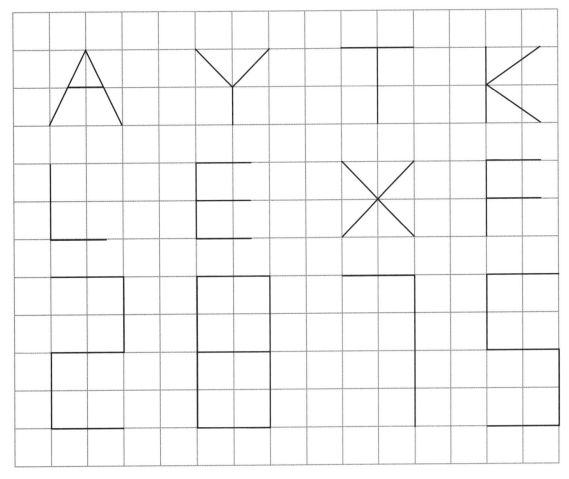

Name all the pairs of perpendicular lines in each figure.

14

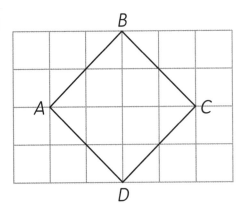

_____

_____

_____

_____

15

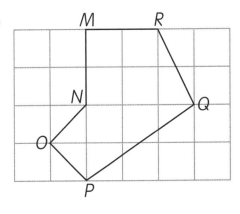

_____

_____

Use a colored pencil to trace a pair of parallel lines on each object.

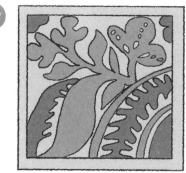

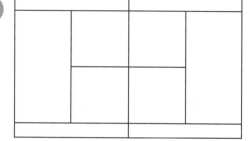

Check (✔) the box if the lines are parallel.
Trace each pair of parallel lines with a colored pencil.
Then, mark these lines with arrowheads (↟↟).

22 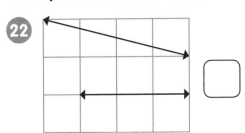 ☐

23 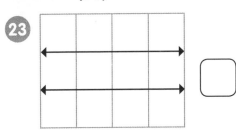 ☐

24 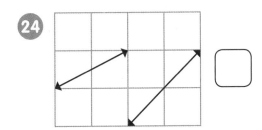 ☐

25 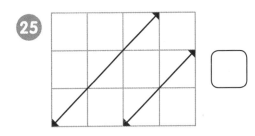 ☐

26 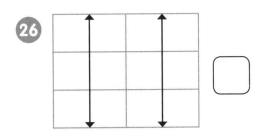 ☐

27 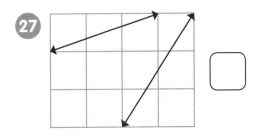 ☐

Trace the pairs of parallel lines with a colored pencil. Mark these lines with parallel arrowheads (↟↟). Circle the letters and numbers that have parallel lines.

28

Name all the pairs of parallel lines in each figure.

29

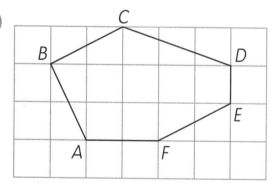

_____

30

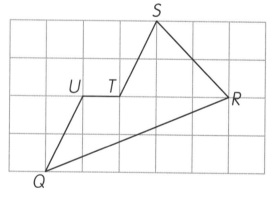

_____

Chapter **12**

Extra Practice and Homework
Angles, Lines, and Two-Dimensional Figures

Activity 3   Polygons

Circle each polygon.

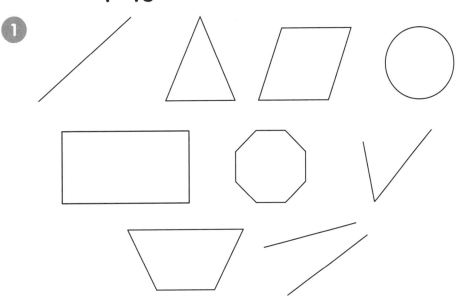

1

Mark the angles in each polygon.
Then, fill in the names of the parts of each polygon.

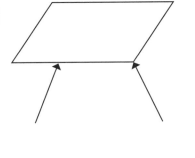

2

_____   _____

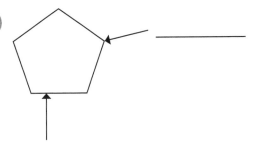

3

_____

Identify each polygon.

 4

_____

5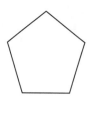

_____

6

_____

7

_____

8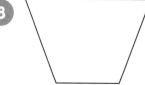

_____

Fill in the table. Then, answer question **10**.

9

Polygons	Number of Sides	Number of Vertices	Number of Angles
square			
hexagon			
triangle			

Polygons	Number of Sides	Number of Vertices	Number of Angles
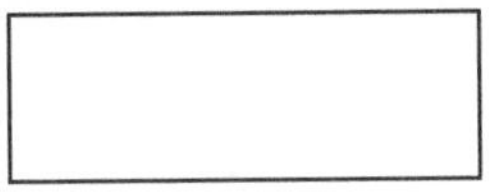 rectangle			
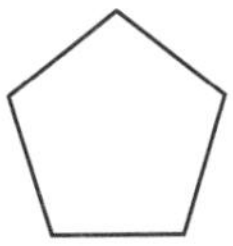 pentagon			
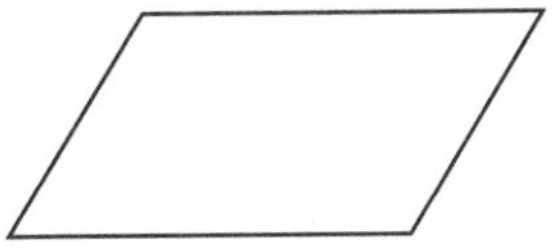 parallelogram			
 rhombus			
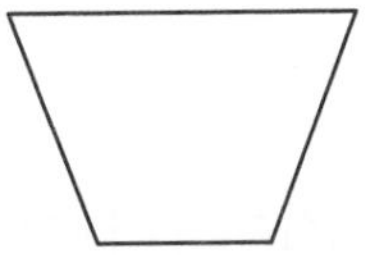 trapezoid			

10 Which figures have the same number of sides, vertices, and angles?

_____

_____

Write "true" or "false" for each statement.

11. A hexagon has seven sides and six angles.   _____

12. All polygons have four sides.   _____

13. All parallelograms, squares, and trapezoids have four angles.   _____

14. A pentagon has six angles.   _____

15. A triangle has two vertices.   _____

16. A parallelogram can be separated into four triangles. _____

17. A rectangle has four right angles.   _____

Fill in each blank.

18. I am a polygon. I have 1 more angle than a rectangle has.
    What am I? _____

19. I am a polygon. I have 1 more side than a pentagon has.
    What am I? _____

20. I am a polygon. I have 1 more vertex than a triangle has.
    What am I? _____

Identify each quadrilateral. Then, explain your answer.

21

This is a _____.

_____

_____

_____

_____

22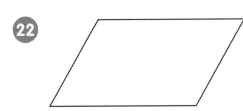

This is a _____.

_____

_____

_____

_____

23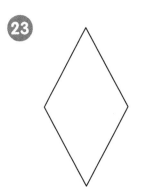

This is a _____.

_____

_____

_____

_____

24 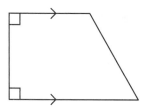   This is a _____.

_____

_____

_____

_____

Write _P_ for a parallelogram, _R_ for a rhombus, or _T_ for a trapezoid on the shapes.

25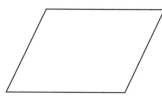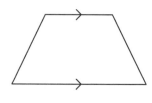

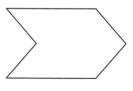 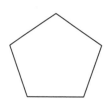 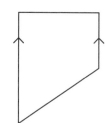

Answer each question.

26 How is a trapezoid different from a parallelogram?

_____

_____

_____

27 How is a trapezoid similar to a parallelogram?

_____

_____

_____

Mathematical Habit 2 **Use mathematical reasoning**

a   Look at the picture below.
   Is *AB* parallel to *CD*?
   Explain.

b   Look at the picture below.
   Is *PQ* perpendicular to *QR*?
   Explain.

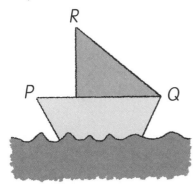

Mathematical Habit 1 Persevere in solving problems

The figure shows a road with parallel kerbs.

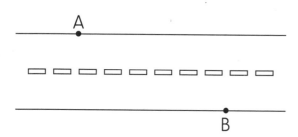

Michelle is standing at Point A and Sara is standing at Point B.
They both want to cross the road.
Draw the shortest route each can take and mark all the right angles ⌐.
Measure the distance along each route.

What can you say about the distance between the parallel lines?

The parallel lines are _____ distance apart.